PUBLIC SPEAKING

Public Speaking Guide for Charismatic and Emotional Presentation, Overcome Fear

(Develop Leadership Level Communication Skills, Social Intelligence and Persuasion Ability)

John Rigby Gregory

Published by Rob Miles

© **John Rigby Gregory**

All Rights Reserved

Communication Skills: Public Speaking Guide for Charismatic and Emotional Presentation, Overcome Fear (Develop Leadership Level Communication Skills, Social Intelligence and Persuasion Ability)

ISBN 978-1-989990-12-4

All rights reserved. No part of this guide may be reproduced in any form without permission in writing from the publisher except in the case of brief quotations embodied in critical articles or reviews.

Legal & Disclaimer

The information contained in this book is not designed to replace or take the place of any form of medicine or professional medical advice. The information in this book has been provided for educational and entertainment purposes only.

The information contained in this book has been compiled from sources deemed reliable, and it is accurate to the best of the Author's knowledge; however, the Author cannot guarantee its accuracy and validity and cannot be held liable for any errors or omissions. Changes are periodically made to this book. You must consult your doctor or get professional medical advice before using any of the suggested remedies, techniques, or information in this book.

Upon using the information contained in this book, you agree to hold harmless the Author from and against any damages, costs, and expenses, including any legal fees potentially resulting from the application of any of the information provided by this guide. This disclaimer applies to any damages or injury caused by the use and application, whether directly or indirectly, of any advice or information presented, whether for breach of contract, tort, negligence, personal injury, criminal intent, or under any other cause of action.

You agree to accept all risks of using the information presented inside this book. You need to consult a professional medical practitioner in order to ensure you are both able and healthy enough to participate in this program.

Table of Contents

INTRODUCTION 1

CHAPTER 1: START FROM THE OUTSIDE—FAKE IT'TIL YOU MAKE IT! 9

CHAPTER 2: EFFECTS OF THE FEAR OF PUBLIC SPEAKING. 13

CHAPTER 3: PRACTICE MAKES PERFECT 16

CHAPTER 4: BE MENTALLY PREPARED 22

CHAPTER 5: YOUR NONVERBAL COMMUNICATION IS A BIG DEAL! 30

CHAPTER 6: THE POWER OF THE SENSES: USING WORDS TO PAINT PICTURES IN YOUR AUDIENCE'S HEADS 47

CHAPTER 7: THE BODY 52

CHAPTER 8: INSPIRATIONAL TED TALKS. 5 TIPS 62

CHAPTER 9: THE KEY ELEMENTS OF SUCCESSFUL PUBLIC SPEAKING 71

CHAPTER 10: THE TOOLS OF THE TRADE 81

CHAPTER 11: HOW TO IMPROVE YOUR BODY LANGUAGE 89

CHAPTER 12: VISUAL AID ACTIVITY 97

CHAPTER 13: WHAT QUALITIES DO YOU NEED? 102

CHAPTER 14: PRINCIPLES OF PUBLIC SPEAKING............. 106

CHAPTER 15: HOW TO FIND A TOPIC OR A SUBJECT TO TALK ABOUT... 111

CHAPTER 16: EVERYBODY HAS A DIFFERENT PERSPECTIVE 115

CHAPTER 17: ◊ SPIRIT & SOURCE................................... 132

CHAPTER 18: HOW TO DELIVER SPEECH 147

CHAPTER 19: FEEDBACK 154

CHAPTER 20: MAKE YOUR TALK INTERESTING............... 159

CHAPTER 21: SHOULD I PREPARE SHORTER VERSIONS? HOW LONG IS TOO LONG FOR A PRESENTATION?......... 175

HOW FAST SHOULD I SPEAK? 176

IS IT OKAY TO READ MY SPEECH?.................................. 177

CHAPTER 22: DO YOU HAVE AN IMPORTANT PRESENTATION?.. 179

CHAPTER 23: STORYTELLING - THE COMPELLING NARRATIVE 184

CHAPTER 24: INFLUENCE THE WORLD ONE SPEECH AT A TIME... 195

CONCLUSION **202**

Introduction

There will always come a time when we have to face a crowd and address them as a group. One of the first opportunities we had to do this was when we were kids at school. Do you still remember the time when you had to make a short presentation or report in front of the class?

Situations like that are truly rattling and they either make you or break you. It either builds your self-confidence or it tears you apart inside insomuch that you lose either the desire or interest (or both) in presenting or speaking to a crowd.

If you're one of the many people who have experienced this or you know of someone who could be going through such an experience then I congratulate you for taking interest in this book. In this book you'll be walking with me through the usual nerve wrecking experience of standing in front of an audience (no matter how big the mob) and delivering a speech.

Not only will you learn the fundamental dynamics of speaking anxiety or presentation anxiety, we'll also look into some easy and practical steps to get over it. Don't worry; we're not going to throw in a lot of technical jargon into the discussion. The fear of presenting to and pleasing an entire crowd is pretty basic for anyone, so why make the solutions harder to understand or implement, right?

I remember the first time I was asked (or actually forced into it is more accurate) to address a huge crowd of people was during high school. One of our professors came in to class, stood in front with a sheet (some sort of check list I guess) and scanned the room.

He was actually looking for someone to fill in for a contestant in a speech competition who couldn't make it that day. I was right smack in front of him so I was practically an easy target that no one can miss. Long story short, I was selected to fill in and I was supposed to give a speech about a social issue of my choice in the next three hours.

Everyone in class congratulated me, gave me pats in the back, and then left. I was stuck in the room trying to figure out what to say let alone figure out a topic to discuss! Thanks for the support guys; none of you guys stayed behind to help me write the speech.

What does a scrawny and slightly hippie kid to do in such a situation? He runs into his comfort zone – rock 'n roll. Since I was to deal with a social issue one of the songs that came to my mind was that Guns 'N Roses song "Civil War."

I thought at the time that it was perfect. The song was about war and other related stuff (not just about the American Civil War). I looked up a lyrics sheet and began to memorize the words – I can sing the song but reciting it was another matter. I then spent the next hour and a half memorizing the lyrics and reciting them in front of a mirror in the boys' room.

I remember the tension and the anxiety I was feeling while waiting for my turn at the stand. Every contestant that went ahead of me was great I guess since they registered nods and smiles from the judges. I couldn't concentrate on what they were saying I was fighting hard to keep my hands from shaking.

Oh, I forgot to mention that there was no podium on the stand, just a mike and a mike stand. You instantly become a spectacle for the crowd. So any sign of nervousness is very visible to the judges and to the crowd.

I wasn't worried about the judges that day. I knew I wouldn't win this one. I was afraid of the crowd. Some of those people in front of me were people I knew but the larger majority was a mob of strangers. I remember putting the lyrics sheet in my pocket and putting my left hand in there with it. That was how I beat the shaking and the chills – that was right about the time when they called my name.

I took a deep breath, walked forward, and spoke the first line: "What we've got here is failure to communicate..."

The crowd erupted and cheered me on! That was insane! With the cheering of the crowd my confidence right on stage grew. As I kept on going I even felt the shaking of my hands dissipate in time. I was communicating to the crowd and they enjoyed what was said. I was able to improvise and throw in a few lines that were completely my own and the students loved it.

As expected, I didn't even make it to the next round of the competition. It was okay for me, I didn't want to go through the nerve wrenching experience anyway. It was good but it wasn't an experience that I want to relish. But the lessons I learned that day stayed with me. Of course, there came a lot of other opportunities for me to provide presentations and speeches to a crowd.

There were a lot of times when I had to address a congregation and explain religious doctrine and discuss spiritual matters. There were plenty of moments when I had to present and explain different marketing plans. There was also a time when I had to teach the English language to a class of foreign students who were learning English as a second language.

I eventually learned how to control my nerves (not that they have completely left me) but I have learned how to manage them. I can now inject a little humor in my presentations and still make it a worthwhile experience for everyone in attendance. I can lay out an hour long lecture and make sure that the entire class remains interested. With confidence I have also learned how to make my public presentations interactive and engaging.

All of that began with just one talk in a contest where I lost. I may not have won the prize in that speech competition so long ago but I was able to win a far greater prize – confidence in front of a crowd.

It took a while before I convinced myself to write a book about the things I learned about public speaking. There are a lot of great books out there that deal with the subject of effective public speaking. But the subject of conquering one's fear of public speaking is one that is really dear to me. That kept on bugging me all these years.

I remember picking up a small booklet in a bookstore one day that dealt with that very subject. It was okay but the meaty part wasn't very convincing. The book basically gave pet answers like using fillers, telling endless stories, and emphasizing that the crowd doesn't care whether you succeeded in your speech or not. It didn't even discuss how to deal with the butterflies your tummy.

I bought that booklet and I did pay the full price of a dollar ninety-nine. I guess that was the worst purchase I made in my life. With such a bad book in my shelf, I was convinced that people needed something better.

This work is the result of me pushing myself to provide anyone with life lessons about public speaking and conquering presentation anxiety. If you're interested in learning practical principles on how to do just that then I invite you to read on.

May the practical lessons on conquering public speaking fear that I learned in my life help you succeed.

Chapter 1: Start From The Outside—Fake It 'Til You Make It!

Fake it 'til you make it, that's what most people say. And you know what? It is actually true. There's this story that you might want to know about. You know Bruce Springsteen, don't you? He's one of the most popular musicians of all time, and is also known to suffer from nerves—especially before performing. But, do his nerves stop him from performing and doing what he does best? Of course not.

You can actually be nervous without being obvious. In short, you have to fake your confidence and eventually, you'll notice you're actually not faking anything anymore, and you're really confident already!

One good way of feeling confident onstage is by looking the part.

You see, people tend to listen to those who look as if they really know what they are talking about, as opposed to those who look like they just dropped by the event for nothing. You don't have to buy extremely expensive clothes, but it would help if you could invest on a few important pieces (slacks, a formal dress, some ties, leather shoes, etc) so that once you get asked to talk in front of an audience, you'd get to show them that you are ready.

It's you who's in charge of making others see you the way you want to be seen. It's you who's in charge of letting others think that you are confident or that you're someone who's just easy to mess with. If you love and accept yourself for who you are, you can expect that others, although they may bash you for it, will still respect you because they can see that you're confident and that you're not someone who can be easily brought down by the words of others.

Meanwhile, if you cannot accept yourself and if you're constantly weighed down by thoughts of how others see you and how you can make others like you, you'll be in big trouble because you really cannot expect that everyone will like you. But, if you love yourself first, it will reflect on the state of your personality and on the way you present yourself to others. People will learn to love you because they know that you love yourself and that you're capable of achieving success.

These days, people are equals. Whether you're an introvert or an extrovert, you have all these opportunities to show the world what you're made of. You have all these chances to learn and grow and that's why it's important for you to understand that you don't have to live in fear; you don't have to let those fears rule over your life. You have to realize that in order to achieve greatness, you have to believe in yourself and everything else will follow.

Try it. Dress up for a certain event that you're invited to and you'd feel like you actually belong there, instead of just feeling like you're just there to pass time. If you want to belong, dress and act like it—and you will.

Of course, it doesn't just end there—after all, this is just the beginning. Once you are already confident with the way you look—you then have to start practicing the way you talk—and you'll learn more about it in the next chapter.

Chapter 2: Effects Of The Fear Of Public Speaking

Being afraid to stand up and speak in front of other people can have several complications that you would not want to face in your life. On the whole, the symptoms of glossophobia, or the fear of public speaking, will hinder many academic, career and social opportunities that come your way.

Here are some scenarios where the fear of public speaking can provide negative effects.

• At school or in class, a student who is afraid to speak out or even answer questions when called will be impeding his or her chances of getting good academic grades.

• At a job interview, an applicant will surely fail to score the job, despite having excellent grades or qualifications, if he is unable to hold himself very well during the series of job interviews that he has to undergo.

• In a corporate setting, an employee cannot expect to convince others to see his point of view in relation to an idea or plan of action if he is unable to explain to them the fine points of his argument and do it with a reassuring confidence. A person who is afraid of facing an audience and speaking before them has doesn't have much hope of ever becoming a leader, or of motivating a group to do something.

Aside from losing so many opportunities in life, other effects of cowering under the fear of public speaking are the loss of one's self-esteem and disruption of his or her life. They tend to avoid any instances or events where they would have to speak in public and, as a result, they can be labeled as being anti-social, or as having poor social skills. This is one reason why glossophobia is also often referred to by experts as a form of social phobia.

It is noticeable how most people tend to develop this fear when they are still very young, or during their formative years. When something becomes ingrained in someone so young, is it still possible to overcome it, despite the fact that it has been embedded in one's psyche for such a long time? Can it still be treated?

The good news is that YES, IT IS POSSIBLE AND IT CAN STILL BE OVERCOME. As a matter of fact, the success rate of overcoming glossophobia is extremely high.

Chapter 3: Practice Makes Perfect

Your preschool teachers will often tell you that practice makes perfect. We often hear those lines when we try to learn how to play an instrument or when we first try to ride a bike. In reality, practice is also crucial to in order to learn the art of public speaking and you will need time and energy in order to master it.

Why practice?

Practicing is not only based on repetition but also in determination. You need to be highly determined in order to master a certain skill. Raw determination is also important when it comes to public speaking since it is where you will draw your confidence. So, if you want to learn how to speak to your audience then you need to make the decision to step outside of your comfort zone.

Of course, in order to step outside your comfort zone you have to be motivated to improve. You need to have something to aim for so that you will be working extra hard. The benefit of learning this valuable skill is different for everyone. Some people try to learn free speech for work while others try to study it in order to improve their relationships. It all depends on what you want to achieve and why you want to learn how to speak in public.

One of the most obvious reasons as to why you might want to improve your public speaking is because you want to get promoted at your job. Yes, getting ahead at your job can be one of your motivators for learning public speaking. For example, employees who can efficiently handle talking to groups of people will most likely become a team leader. Those who show confidence while in the office will most likely become a manager. Even in supermarkets wherein sellers will be promoted to a supervisor just because they are able to motivate their fellow employees.

The next motivation for public speaking is empowerment. Everybody wants to follow a leader. A leader is confident, he knows what to say during a crisis, he works under pressure, he has the power to control the crowd through his words, and he knows a lot about the world. In a group setting, those who know how to lead will always be nominated as the leader.

Of course, the most obvious reason may be to improve in social situations. People who are gifted with the art of public speaking are often the ones who are attractive to others. People who are also good when it comes to speaking with other people will most likely have more friends than those who are generally shy.

Work smart not hard

Have you ever heard of the line "work smart not hard?" This line is not only applicable to your current occupation but also in public speaking.

How to practice public speaking

Now that you are highly motivated to improve your public speaking, the next step is to learn what to practice. There are several ways for you to practice public speaking and it all depends on your system. Of course, you will need to focus on the topic that you will be presenting to the crowd so that you will not falter at the last minute. Many people panic when they are in front of the audience simply because they forget what their topic is. That is why you will need to practice constantly in order to memorize and summarize your talking points. Remember, never rely too much on memorization, instead you need to focus on the main points of your topic. The main points will help you to go impromptu if you forget some of the lines in your topic.

Once you have composed your topic and you have written down its outline then it is now time to practice. You can either start your speech while in front of a mirror or you can use your family or close friends as your test audience. Again, this all depends on how comfortable you are.

Try to start your speech with a short introduction. Some famous speakers try to start their speech by cracking a joke to lighten the mood with the crowd. This actually depends on your crowd. If your future audience will be the board members of your company then you need to make your introduction short and concise.

Once you start, remember that you are talking with a crowd so learn to speak slowly and clearly. Never falter when it comes to your topic and be sure to look your audience in the eyes. This technique will enable you to master the feel of the room when it comes to public speaking. You also need to learn how to pace yourself while in front of the crowd.

Chapter 4: Be Mentally Prepared

Needless to say, the most important thing that you can do before any public speech or presentation is to become mentally prepared. While much of the anxiety of public speaking can be attributed to physiological causes and general shyness, the truth is that it is also directly linked to how prepared a person is. Overall, the more prepared you are, the less anxious you will be. There are several ways in which you can prepare for an event, including practice, organization and increasing your familiarity with the subject at hand. This chapter will address four different methods of mental preparation that will significantly reduce stress and anxiety, as well as increase the quality of your performance in overall.

Organize Your Material

Many studies have been done to determine the most effective strategies regarding business and professional practices. One of the most common conclusions is that the more chaotic an environment, the more prone it is to failure. This affects not only groups of people but individuals as well. When a person is disorganized, they fail to fulfill their full potential no matter what the given situation might be. However, when a person takes extra time and effort to organize such things as their schedule, tasks they need to perform and other such elements they increase their chances of success exponentially. Furthermore, increased organization has been shown to significantly decrease stress and anxiety, thereby making both individuals and groups of people more effective as a result. Subsequently, in order to reduce the anxiety and stress of a public presentation it is vital that you organize your material.

One way to organize material is to reduce the actual amount of material you have to deal with. More often than not people think that the more material they have is, the more prepared they are. Unfortunately, this can lead to clutter, confusion and a general sense of chaos that only serves to undermine the individual's performance. Too much stuff is never a good thing, so eliminate all the excess right from the start. A good way to do this is to transfer information from various sources onto a single reference sheet, thereby streamlining your load to a more manageable level. Furthermore, you can organize the material you are covering by reducing it to bullet points, thereby condensing large blocks of information into smaller 'bites' of information that you can expand upon with your own personal experience and knowledge.

Focus On What You Know

Another main reason why so many people struggle with giving public presentations is that they often feel out of their depth with regard to the material itself. This can be a real problem in the event that you are giving a speech to a group of people who are well versed on the subject of your presentation. Any time you feel as though you are competing with those you are speaking to it will only increase the stress and anxiety you feel. Therefore, only ever give a presentation when the subject is something that you already know a whole lot about. The more knowledgeable you are, the more comfortable you will be with speaking in front of others.

This proves especially true in the event that members of the group you are speaking to ask questions about the topic of your presentation. If you are speaking about something you don't know much about you will probably be caught off guard by questions you don't have the answers to. Although you won't necessarily be expected to have all the answers, you should at least have most of them. Therefore, make sure you only give presentations on things you have a deep understanding of. This will prevent awkward moments where you appear unprepared and out of your depth. It can also serve to make the experience more fun as most people enjoy talking about what they understand or are passionate about.

Keep It Simple

Perhaps the number one piece of advice given by successful public speakers is to always keep it simple. This goes hand in hand with always being prepared, as simplicity prevents chaos and the stress and anxiety that result from it. However, rather than referring to the physical material, keeping it simple refers to the presentation itself. Most people feel that a successful presentation has to cover a wide range of information. This can result in a person trying to discuss too much material in the time given, moving from point to point without taking a breath in-between. Not only does this add to the stress of the presenter, but it also leaves the audience feeling overwhelmed as they are bombarded with countless facts and information, proving more than they can make sense of.

The fact is that a simple presentation is better for everyone involved. Not only is it easier for the speaker to talk about six or seven points instead of twenty or thirty, but it is also more beneficial for those listening to the presentation as well. After all, if you were introduced to four or five people the chances of you remembering their names would be better than if you were introduced to fifteen or twenty people. The same holds true for any introduction of information. Keeping it simple makes it easier for you to stay focused and on track and it makes the presentation more educational and memorable for the audience.

Practice Makes Perfect

Anyone who makes a living as an actor or stage performer will tell you that the key to being successful is practice, practice, practice. This philosophy holds true for any form of presentation, whether it's reciting lines in a play, acting in a movie or simply giving a public speech. As the axiom states, "Practice makes perfect." Therefore, if you really want to reduce the stress and anxiety of public speaking make sure that you practice your presentation over and over again until it becomes second nature. The more familiar you are with the presentation is, the less afraid you will be of getting it wrong.

While some people content themselves with practicing their speech in their mind, the truth is that practicing it out loud is far more effective. There are several reasons for this. First is the fact that you will become more comfortable hearing yourself as you practice your speech out loud. Many people feel self-conscious when they hear themselves speaking, and this can cause increased stress and anxiety at the time of the presentation. However, if you become familiar with the sound of your own voice you can avoid that stress, making the experience easier as a result. Second, by practicing the speech out loud you can discover any parts that might be tricky, either because of word choice or just because of how things are arranged. By practicing your presentation out loud you can discover these pitfalls in advance, thereby eliminating them from your public performance.

Chapter 5: Your Nonverbal Communication Is A Big Deal!

Many people assume that one's presentation begins the moment one takes the podium, but I am here to tell you that you are making a big mistake if you buy into this train of thought. The reality is that your presentation begins the moment you take a step onto the grounds of the venue. Why? Because people are going to be checking you out as soon as they see you. You are your product, which means that you must put on your professional hat before you even leave the house. Let's address several areas of nonverbal communication and examine what you can do in each area to maximize your ability to use them to your advantage.

Grooming / Hygiene

Chances are that unless your presentation involves a webinar, you are going to be very near other people the day of your presentation. This means that it is in your best interest to clean up and dress up so that you increase the likelihood that you will be viewed favorably.

Take a shower the morning of your presentation if possible, or at least the night before. I know that there are certain things that I must do the day of a presentation to ensure that I look as good as I can. I don't want someone I meet before or after my presentation walking away and thinking, "Man, that guy should have cleaned the dirt under his fingernails!" You may be laughing as you read that, but I am just making the point that it's important to eliminate any hygiene issue that could potentially cause others to think negatively of you. And, oh, yes: brush your teeth, floss, and keep a tin of mints on your person. Nothing can kill a first impression faster than bad breath.

Attire

The quality of your physical presence is largely determined by what you wear and how you wear it. Different presentations call for different clothing, which means you must know the occasion that is bringing your audience together so that you can make strategic decisions regarding your attire for the day. Obviously, if you have been asked to speak about the benefits of ostrich farming at an outdoor barbecue for rural entrepreneurs just outside of Oklahoma City, it would probably not be a great idea to wear a tailored suit and your favorite $300 dress shoes. Do your homework, find out as much as you can about the venue and your audience, and then choose your clothing for the day. Your goal is to look professional and approachable.

If the occasion does call for professional attire, make sure your clothes are pressed and your shoes are shined.

Nothing can kill a first impression quicker than an unkempt outfit. Take the time to sharpen your appearance. The time you put into your style will not only impress your audience, but it will also make you feel more confident.

Body Language

Entire books have been written on the significance of body language. Often, the messages you send nonverbally to others ends up saying much more than the words that come out of your mouth. The way presenters stand, sit, walk, shake hands, and use eye contact can either enhance their likeability and credibility, or cause their intended audience to turn off their attention shortly after, or even before, the presentation begins.

Movement

It is critical for presenters to remember that the way they move during presentations is going to be interpreted by audience members, and whether those interpretations work for, or against presenters can be controlled. Here are some valuable tips for using your body when making a presentation:

• One of the most important tips regarding body movement involves your face. *Your smile* is your most potent tool in terms of nonverbal communication and you should practice and learn to use it liberally during a presentation. Presenters who smile often are generally viewed as more competent and confident. More importantly, people who smile tend to be more likeable than those who don't, and if your audience likes you, they are more likely to pay attention to your message.

• *Keep your arms and your chest open*. Crossing your arms over your chest sends a nonverbal message that you are feeling insecure or closed off from your audience. Not only will an open posture help your audience view you more favorably, but it will also help you to breathe easier and feel more at ease during your presentation.

• Whether you are standing or sitting during your presentation, pay close attention to your *posture*. No matter how informal your presentation, your goal is to appear professional, alert, and energized. The best way to convey this appearance is to sit or stand up straight. A straight posture will also help you feel confident and will improve your ability to project your voice.

• When speaking to a group while standing, presenters have a certain amount of space that allows them to move around. *Take advantage of the space allotted to you*. Don't be afraid to come out from behind the podium and approach the audience, or move to the left or to the right. When you move, you attract your listeners' attention, which serves to keep them interested.

When you move, however, move with a purpose. Come closer to the audience when you wish to emphasize a point, or move to three different parts of your speaking area to address three different points of your argument. It is rarely a good idea to place yourself in a position where your audience members cannot see you, so refrain from moving behind them. I attended a presentation recently where the man was moving around so much that he made everyone in the room nervous. Obviously, that is not your goal!

• If you are using visual aids, such as slides or a PowerPoint presentation, *physically point and look toward key messages on slides* that you wish to emphasize. Your audience will follow your lead and look there as well.

• When someone from the audience asks a question directed at you, *nod* as you listen to them. This simple head gesture will send a nonverbal validation to questioners which will make them feel more comfortable.

- After someone has asked a question of you, it is a good practice to *repeat the question out loud*. This serves two purposes: it allows everyone in the audience to hear what was asked, and it allows questioners to confirm that you correctly understood what they asked.

Eye Contact

Making eye contact with listeners is a strong tool that can add so much to a presentation. The use of effective eye contact is a learned skill for most people, however, and must be practiced in order to reap the greatest rewards for using it. Here's a list of reasons that eye contact is so critical in presentations:

- A presenter's effective use of the eyes to connect with listeners will increase his likeability and credibility. Making eye contact with audience members will also give them a sense of the presenter's level of confidence about the topic that is being shared.
- When presenters engage individual audience members using their eyes, listeners are more apt to keep looking at them. This is important because if listeners are looking at the presenter, they are more than likely listening to what is being said. Once an audience member looks away from the speaker, they have disengaged and it is entirely possible that they will tune out the rest of the presentation.
- Effective use of eye contact sends a message to the audience that the presenter believes in the message being conveyed and that they are confident about the information being shared.
- When presenters make eye contact with members of the audience, they are inviting listeners to actively engage

nonverbally. It won't happen all the time, but listeners will often respond to eye contact by offering a nod or a facial expression that gives a cue to the presenter as to the level of acceptance of the topic by the listener. When a nonverbal message is received by the presenter, this gives the presenter the option to respond verbally in order to validate the listener's message.

- A presenter's response to a nonverbal message conveyed by a listener shows that the presenter is paying attention and that he cares about the response, which can enhance the audience's positive feelings about the presentation.
- Effective use of eye contact can give listeners a strong sense of active participation in the presentation, which can only serve to increase their attention.
- Presenters who master effective eye contact find that it increases their own self-confidence. In addition, it allows them to better concentrate and give a stronger presentation.

Techniques for Mastering Eye Contact

Establishing eye contact in small gatherings is fairly easy. Just remember that if you are addressing a small group, make sure you try to establish eye contact with each person in the room, rather than just the people sitting directly in front of you, or the perceived leader of the group. Eye contact makes your audience feel like they are important to you, which should be your goal in any speaking environment.

The practice, however, is a bit more complicated when one is speaking to larger groups. Try to establish eye contact with as many people in the room as possible and try to do it in a random fashion. One should have strong mastery over his presentation to pull off making eye contact 90-95% of a presentation but that should be the goal.

How long should your eye contact last with listeners? The answer to this question may depend on how many people are listening to your presentation, but a good rule of thumb is to stay with one person as you speak one phrase or one sentence. Then, move to another person. I have attended presentations where the speaker spent too much time looking at me to the point where I felt uncomfortable. And, some people are uncomfortable with anyone looking at them for any length of time. If you get the sense that an audience member is not comfortable with your eye contact, simply look away and move to the next person.

Voice
As a trained oral communicator, your instrument of delivery is your voice. To get the most out of your voice, you must practice using it regularly just like you would practice any other instrument. Speakers who take time to learn how to

use the elements of sound as they speak to their audiences will be better able to hold the attention of listeners and add interest to their presentations. Here are some tips that should help you use your voice as one of your most powerful presentation tools:

1. *Use the volume and pitch of your speech* to hold the attention of your audience. Of course, you always want to be speaking with enough volume so that everyone in the room can hear what you are saying, but you can increase the volume to emphasize those key points that you are trying to get across to your listeners. Pitch refers to the range of high and low tones you use with your voice. A speaker can also use pitch to emphasize words or phrases in a speech to drive home important points. For example, read the following sentences out loud and emphasize the underlined word in each sentence to see how pitch can change the meaning of a sentence:

- "▇didn't drive Jennifer and Tom to the prom" (perhaps someone else drove them?).
- "I ▇▇▇▇drive Jennifer and Tom to the prom" (speaker is emphatically denying driving the couple to the prom).
- "I didn't ▇▇▇▇Jennifer and Tom to the prom" (perhaps the speaker walked Jennifer and Tom to the prom).
- "I didn't drive ▇▇▇▇▇and Tom to the prom" (speaker drove Tom and someone else).
- "I didn't drive Jennifer and Tom to the ▇▇▇▇" (speaker drove Jennifer and Tom somewhere else).

2. Pay attention to the *pace and rhythm* of your speech. Audiences are going to be either positively or negatively affected depending on how you handle these variables. If you speak too slowly, or speak slowly without purpose, you risk losing the attention of the audience. If you speak too quickly, your audience will wonder why you are in such a hurry and may assume that you have a more important engagement following your

presentation that you are trying to get to as soon as possible.

A monotonic rhythm, one in which the speaker uses the same pace throughout his speech, will potentially make listeners think you are simply going through the motions instead of being invested in what you are talking about. Change up your rhythm by pausing for emphasis on occasion, and by speaking slower for emphasis.
3. Utilize the *power of silence* in your presentations. New speakers are often deathly afraid of silence because they think that listeners will think they are lost or do not know what to say next. Speakers who are trained in the art of public speaking realize that silence may be used quite effectively as a bridge between ideas being discussed, to create suspense, and for emphasis. Don't be afraid of silence. Audiences often appreciate it because it gives them time to absorb the message being presented.

4. Work on the *quality* of your voice. Practice using your voice and breathe from your abdomen. Keep your vocal chords hydrated by drinking water (other liquids, such as soda or coffee, may serve to dry out your vocal chords). Pay attention to your posture by sitting and standing with your back straight when you are speaking. This will allow the air from your abdomen to flow unobstructed through your vocal chords.

To reiterate, never underestimate the importance of nonverbal communication, whether you are making a presentation, in a meeting, or on a date. Take time to observe nonverbal cues put forth by the people around you; I believe you will find that the messages people deliver without even speaking can be very powerful, indeed.

Questions to Ponder:

1. One can communicate nonverbally in a lot of different ways. What parts of nonverbal communication have you mastered?
2. How can you improve your nonverbal communication?

Chapter 6: The Power Of The Senses: Using Words To Paint Pictures In Your Audience's Heads

There's a saying when it comes to story writing: show, don't tell. That means, instead of telling your reader outright that so-and-so is a *bad guy*, write a scene in which his actions reveal his lack of moral fiber instead.

When your story *telling*, the principle remains the same.

In last chapter's example monomyth, the speaker does more than just *telling* his audience that the sunrise was something beautiful. Instead, he first lets them reach that conclusion on their own.

He describes the lovely colors that he saw that morning, painting a picture of a lovely sunrise for his audience to enjoy in their own mind's eye.

Likewise, in the midst of --his "ordeal," he never outright tells the audience that he's miserable. Instead, he tells them certain details that add up to form the picture of a miserable person.

If you want to really connect with your audience, this is how it's done. The less selfless you are in your manner of storytelling, the better. Literally share *your experience* with the audience.

Research shows that after just a few minutes of passive observation, a person's brain switches over into the "alpha" state of mind. In this state, a listener's subconscious is "exposed" and they are much more vulnerable to suggestion.

Their higher functions or reasoning and critical thinking are diminished, their guard is let down, and—at least, initially—they're along for the ride whether they like it or not. It's your job to keep them in that state with plenty of passive brain stimulation.

How to do that? With good storytelling, of course. More specifically, with *vivid* storytelling that stimulates your audience's imaginations. When their imaginations are engaged, they'll be less critical of your message, and they'll also be more open to new ideas.

While relaying your story, give each audience member's senses something to chew on. Again, share *your experience.* Tell them how you broke out into goosebumps. How your stomach dropped. How a chill ran up your spine.

Pepper your narrative with sensory-rich statements such as these, and you're guaranteed to captivate your audience on a whole new level.

Some Simple but Effective Sensory-Rich Angles to Consider:

- Describe physical reactions that you had to the event. "I just blinked." "My stomach dropped." "My throat closed up." This is a powerful tactic for putting the listener in your shoes.

Everybody's experienced these involuntary physical reactions at some point in their lives. Your audience's mind, therefore, is already wired to associate these things with certain stimuli.

- Talk about what your hands or other parts of your body were doing while the event was taking place. Don't tell them you were mad, tell them how your hands balled up into fists.

  Don't say you were afraid, talk about how you could feel your fingers trembling. Don't say that a person in the story looked impatient, describe how they were tapping their foot on the ground at sixty miles per hour.

- Experiment with the present tense as you tell your story. You may have noticed that the example monomyth shifted tense like this towards the peak of the message. Such a change is much less obvious in a verbal presentation.

Don't say "and then our boat went under," describe the process of your shipwreck as if it were unfolding before your eyes right now.

Talk about how you "look down and there's water up to your ankles out of nowhere." Act as if whatever you're talking about was going on in the present.

This is another useful technique for inserting your audience into the cockpit of your story.

Chapter 7: The Body

You have only two tools with which to communicate a message—your body and your voice. Of course, you can use visual aids and props of various sorts, but it's you yourself who is communicating a message. So it's imperative that you make the best use of the two tools that you can.

Let's take the body first.

Some very practical advice:
1. Don't cross your arms and/or huddle into yourself. Either of these two positions broadcasts that you don't want to be approached, maybe because you hate the situation you're in or else you're terrified. Doing both at the same time is warning the audience: Stay away from me; I mean it!

2. Don't slouch. A lazy posture suggests that you don't care about your audience or else you'd make a better effort at communicating effectively. Yes, and nonverbal communication definitely has a big influence on an audience.

3. It's great to move from one space on the stage or floor when changing from one major point to another or for directly addressing different parts of the audience. However, don't pace randomly, or soon the audience may be paying much more attention to the walking back and forth than to what you're saying verbally. Pacing suggests unease or downright nervousness.

4. Don't use jerky or too small gestures, or the audience will likely start laughing. Similarly, don't do planned gestures because often they come across as phony or mechanical.

5. Don't make unusual moves, like constantly brushing your hair from your forehead or pushing your glasses up on

the nose. This too distracts from the overall presentation.

Nonverbal Communication

Something you should keep in mind as you're getting ready to give a talk is that communication definitely is not a one-way street. Certainly, the feedback you receive during your presentation is not as direct as it is during a conversation, but it still is present. It still is important, and you need to pay attention to how the audience reacts.

Unless the auditorium in which you're speaking is too dark for you to see the audience, you need to be aware of how they're reacting. Are they fidgety? Do they have puzzled looks on their faces? Are they paying attention, and do they seem interested in what you're saying? If it's the first reaction, you can be almost certain your presentation is going well. But if they're fidgety, things are not as they should be. Are the listeners bored? If so you'd better change what you're saying or how you're saying it. Maybe you're going into too much detail for an audience that knows little about the subject. In other words, you may have caused a mental overload so that they can no longer concentrate. In that case, you should know your material well enough to skip a lot of the detail and concentrate on the more major points. If they're puzzled, you can even mention something about it. "I see a few of you are frowning. So I'll try to make things a little clearer. And then if I still haven't clarified things well enough, we'll set aside a few moments for questions." You smile. "Okay, let's try again."

The point is that you should pay attention to what the audience is telling you nonverbally and adjust the presentation accordingly. Our bodies are constantly communication our thoughts and feelings. We communicate much more nonverbally than with words.

How do we use our bodies to communicate? Through facial expression, posture and carriage, gestures, and eye contact. This means we have to pay attention to what we are communicating. As mentioned, if we slouch in front of an audience, we communicate things we probably didn't have in mind—negative feelings in the audience. "The speaker must not care about the audience or he would put more effort into the speech." "Didn't his parents ever tell him to stand up straight?" "Why should I even listen?" Standing up straight, but comfortably, can communicate confidence, straightforwardness, and ease with the situation. Just as we learn to speak by imitating, we learn as infants and children what certain nonverbal signs convey. Yet even knowing these signs, we still often give ourselves away by broadcasting feelings that we would just as soon others didn't pick up. Overall, we've learned what certain gestures mean—things like nodding and shrugging. But there are many other behaviors we need to be aware of as public speakers. These behaviors often give more "meaning" to our speaking in front of others than words do.

Gestures

Gestures can be a very important part of a speech because they fulfill many functions. They can point up something; they can emphasize a point you're making, and they can liven the speech so that the audience is more likely to pay attention.

There are four types of gestures:
1. Those that direct or indicate;
2. Those that describe or illustrate;
3. Those that express or emphasize;
4. Those that are meant to be private.

You use the first one, of course, to help give directions, to point out something, or to indicate something—possibly a part of a chart or other visual aid you're using.

The second type is less exact, though when accompanied with words, it is usually self-apparent. "The rattlesnake was only this far away," we say and spread our arms. We circle our ear with our index finger to imply that something or someone is crazy. The third type is for emphasis. We shrug to indicate something doesn't matter. We throw our hands into the air to protest something, or we shake a finger at someone. These often indicate how we're feeling, but often don't mean so much if you don't accompany them with words. You can use any or all of these in your speeches. But you should never use the fourth type in a speech. This communicates things you don't' want your audience to know...unless maybe you're giving a humorous talk. Private gestures include things like tapping a pencil against the podium, which shows impatience, or pursing our lips in disapproval. Much of the time we don't even realize we're doing this sort of thing.

Gestures can greatly enhance a speech, or they can be detrimental. To some people gestures are natural. You can see this any time you're in public since, as the saying goes, some people "talk with their hands." But it's not uncommon for beginning speakers to use gestures that appear inhibited. That is, they're very small, or else they're done at waist level rather than expansively.

If at first, you find that it's difficult for you to use gestures, it's better not to call attention to those that are less than what they should be. That means that you may have a difficult time using gesture to begin with, but don't worry about it. In fact, don't even think about it. Generally, the more experience a speaker has and the more confidence, the more and better the gestures.

Gestures also should fit the size of the audience. You wouldn't use expansive gestures if you were speaking in front of a group of fifteen or twenty people, and you wouldn't use smaller gestures with hundreds of members in the audience.

Eye Contact

Eye contact is important, particularly in a small audience where it's easy for the audience to see if a speaker really is talking to them and not to some mythical person or audience far away. Eye contact tells the audience that you have something you really want to communicate, that you believe enough in your message that you aren't afraid to tell them. It gives more veracity to the talk, and tells the audience that you are comfortable speaking to them.

Moving from Spot to Spot

Movement from one place to another on the stage or speaker's area also is important. It helps the audience stay awake and interested, whereas someone who stands still for a talk can made the audience lose interest or let their minds wander.

Facial Expression

Facial expression is important in communicating mood. If you laugh or smile, for instance, it indicates what you're about to say is humorous or funny. A stern expression can convey disapproval or a no-nonsense message. The facial expression backs up what you say. So try to make sure that the facial expressions you use communicate what you want them to—not timidity at giving the speech, nor impatience with co-workers who aren't understanding you.

Chapter 8: Inspirational Ted Talks. 5 Tips

1. Get proverbial with TED talks

Knowing about the matter in question is more crucial before the method of implementation is made familiar. TED Talks are a platform for speakers conveying well crafted thoughts and dreams in less than or sometimes a little more than 18 minutes.

Many of the readers may feel inquisitive about the logic of these 18 minutes. The communication framework of TED connotes that the respective audience is competent enough to grasp the message as they are concentrated towards only one message being delivered.

The short duration of time is the basic feature of TED talks. The duration is not the characteristic which makes the message effective; it is the subject matter which governs the utility and effectiveness of TED talks. Even a few seconds are enough to sweep the ground.

2. Craft an idea

The idea can be the basic theme of revolution, to make your TED talk exclusive. There can be varied ways of making the ideas striking and conspicuous. Some ways include providing an overall exclusive idea, or providing an altogether new way of some hard and firm beliefs, which makes the audience compelled towards a new way of thinking.

Sometimes the idea is not that exclusive rather the way of presentation is highly exclusive. Whichever your case is, make it solid and attractive so that the audience gets caught in the charisma of the representation and argumentation style.

Many of you may think that TED talks demand for the speaker to be a multitasking expert, who needs to have lots of intellectual capability. The core idea is the nature of the idea. If you are about to deliver a TED talk, you need to have a thorough search and grasp over the topic. You need to be in contact with some experts who can guide you well. But one major point is the accuracy of information.

Whatever you are about to convey to your audience, you must be accurate as your major priority. No matter you provide a few facts, but these facts must be based on reality and accurate assessment of beliefs. It is because TED talks are based on the audience's firm belief on the speaker.

So make the factual and decisive claims. If your audience is listening to you it does not mean that you can say them whatever you want. The decoders are now smart enough to screen the viable and reliable information from the whole message. So screen it yourself, before the audience does it for you. Moreover providing the honest and factual claims will make up your reputation as an honest and concrete TED speaker. So your repute is in your own control.

Compose others believe in you and it demands honesty and integrity from the very beginning.

Not every raw thought can serve the purpose of TED talks. So make it the best. Not every though, it is the attractive idea. So certain specific characteristics are needed to make the idea worth deliverable. The idea must be based on facts, having some exclusive paradigm to think upon.

3. Get Prepared With a Script

The art of TED talks does not follow any scientific rule of thumb. Every circumstance entails a different challenge. So to craft your script you need to keep this in mind

Start by having a clearer analysis of the audience. Not every audience demands for the same script. Keep in mind the demographic and intellect of the audience.

The layout of your script must be an invisible scheme, which is a secret between you and your mind. Although the script forms a systematic background, but the real charisma of the script must be interpreted through the exclusive speaking styles and powers.

Detailing each and every component without any clear demarcation is the real success of the script. Make it your personal and hidden tool which is formulated and practiced in your mind.

The introduction can either make or break the entire TED talks. The introduction must be captivating. Do not overburden your introduction with figures and statistic. An introduction swarming with your own introduction can also be fatiguing and boring. So make two or three crunch lines in your introduction.

There are number of introduction recipes available, but the one you may need, depends upon the particular scenario and the exclusive audience. Never try to copy the ideas of others. The scheme which has proven to be successful in one TED talk may create disasters in other situations. So even if you want to copy some one's style, copy it in some innovative way.

If there are certain clash of beliefs or some other parallel approaches towards your idea, try to address them sensibly and respectfully. If there are opposite beliefs do not hide them under the rug. Face them with valor, because hiding them will strike your reputation if any of your members in the audience is clear about the.

It is not the stance of questioning; somewhat it is an ethical concern for the spokesman to address these clashes.

4. Keep Practicing

Although there is no scientific rule of thumb for any TED talk yet like all other fields it demands hard work and an efficient practice. Construct yourself your own administrator. One elite factor is to make you n time. Practicing will aid you to make your TED talk restricted to 18 minutes.

Another factor is to practice the posture. Imagine yourself in front of an audience. The posture can also portray a far effective message for the audience.

If your body language is confident and illustrative, you are almost done with conquering the minds of your audience. Once the TED talk gets scheduled, try to manage for stage rehearsal it will help you to give away the fear and have a balanced emotional state.

5. Use the appropriate medium as the visual aids

As we discussed in the communication cycle that the decoders and the respective audience plays a pivotal role in selection of many different aspects.

One of them is the visual aids. Sometimes a PowerPoint presentation with static text is enough to deliver the best TED. In some scenarios you may need the help of a number of video aids to convey the subject matter more accurately and clearly.

Keep one thing in common that the audience must be familiar with the chosen aid. Make sure that the eighteen minutes are utilized conveying the message rather than making the audience familiar with the aid and techniques being in process.

Chapter 9: The Key Elements Of Successful Public Speaking

There are some basic principles required when it comes to speaking in public. It is important that you understand these and think about them. By doing so, it gives you the perfect foundation blocks on which to build your confidence and to understand what is required of a good public speaker. As a reminder, at the end of the module, we will list the 7 basic principles but let's discuss them first.

Don't Chase Perfection

Chasing perfection is a serious flaw. If you practice sufficiently, you should not worry that your speech will be anything less than good. Even if you make minor mistakes, your audience are unlikely to detect them unless they know the subject matter well and you have incorrect information. The odd error — for a split moment, hesitating when you have forgotten your words, may just make you appear human and providing you have prepared well, you will continue regardless. A split-second of hesitation may seem like a long time when up on a stage but, you learn from these mistakes.

Perfection is one of those impossible states to achieve as there are always ways to improve things and you end up chasing the impossible. It makes far more sense to focus on the message that you are imparting. How can you get the message across to the audience, so they understand it in the best way? Also, it is important to remember that the audience will not know your script, so, you could completely miss out lines and if it still made sense they would not notice. People rarely attend an event looking for perfection, they tend to relate to people who come across as being warm and human.

Visualization is a very powerful technique. To utilize this technique, you visualize the perfect scenario, and, create an outcome that embeds itself into your sub-conscious mind. Top sportsmen use this tactic a lot and it works. They don't just imagine making a home run, they see it and feel it. Visualize yourself successfully delivering a speech, do this every day and eventually, it will just become what you naturally expect. It even reduces nerves. Your mind will act as if it already knows what will happen and this will reduce your nerves.

How You Perceive and How They Perceive

To become a good public speaker, you need to learn how to relax. The perception that you must be this polished professional who is grammatically correct and flows through paragraph after paragraph without a single flaw or error is false. The public do not have that perception of you either. They will connect to those who are relaxed. They want to believe in you and to some degree, be entertained by you. Or, they want to learn something from you. They will focus more on your words when you're interesting and confident.

Helpful tip

If you can have a relaxed conversation with two of your friends, then you are also capable of having the same conversation with 2000 people.

Even though your intention is not for perfection, it pays to practice. Practice gives you confidence, it helps you to understand your timings which is incredibly important. To be successful in almost anything, it requires repetitive action. The more you practice, the better you become. Practicing your speech in front of family and friends will certainly aid your confidence levels and, you must believe that you can do the same professional standard when on the stage.

The most interesting speeches are those where the speaker personalizes his communication with stories and facts that relate to the topic but which also, contain some humor. The reason this works so well is because people want to hear about real people that they can relate to. Personal triumphs and mistakes will warm the audience to you, and by sharing life stories you will also relax yourself.

Tip
 Remember that your goal is to benefit the audience in some way. The focus should be about them

Don't Leave Them Hanging but DO Leave Them Wanting. ☐

Remember some of the speeches that you attended yourself? How many captivated you from start to finish? Equally, how many speeches or presentations have you longed to be over? What makes one speech stand out from the other? This is worth considering because you can learn a lot from other speakers.

It is important to add structure to your speech so that the listener is always waiting for the next sentence. If you are delivering a speech that is both entertaining and being delivered in a warm and confident manner then, this helps the whole speech slot into place naturally. Sometimes, shorter speeches work better as it is easier to hold the attention of the audience but of course, you might not have complete control over that if you have a certain time slot to fill. A shorter speech which is filled with information can leave the audience wanting more.

Prior to the event, you need to consider how you are going to appear to your audience. It is important that you feel relaxed and so, it is best to wear something that you feel good in and clothes that tell the audience something about you. If you do not usually wear a suit in everyday life, you may feel awkward suddenly wearing one in front of an audience. If there is a dress code, then, get used to wearing the outfit in advance. All these things are important, and it is much better to prepare yourself beforehand and allow yourself to get used to small changes like this.

The more you know about the event, the better you can be prepared. Find out beforehand if you are going to be using a podium and if there are steps leading up to the stage. Will you be at the same level as the audience or slightly looking down on them. Will you be announced, or do you have to walk on as soon as someone else finishes? Knowing these things will benefit you and afford a sense of control, because the last thing you need on the night of the event is to have your focus shifted.

So, it pays to think about these 7 elements of public speaking as it forms a good starting point for your journey into public speaking.

Don't chase perfection
- Visualize success
- How you perceive and how they

perceive
- Practice
- Entertain
- Don't leave them hanging
- Preparing

Public speaking may not be easy all the time but, it is not as difficult as many people think. It is something that almost everyone can do, and almost all of us, even if somewhat reluctantly, will need to make a public speech at some point. Whether it is at a family event such as a wedding or at a corporate event, the rules are the same. If you know your subject, this will give you some confidence and you can practice delivering your speech in a warm and entertaining way.

In the next module, we are going to explore further ways to build confidence and to learn how to create a connection with your audience.

Chapter 10: The Tools Of The Trade.

By the time you complete the first two steps of the development of your public speaking presentation, you will have a huge amount of information that will help you refine what you are going to talk about and how you will talk about it that day. You should be congratulated because these early steps of learning every possible detail about the public speaking event are steps that many people never do and that is why those public speakers flounder.

One of the best tricks for learning how to become an outstanding public speaker is to watch people who do it all the time and learn the methods they use to do well in front of a group of people. One thing you will notice is that very few speakers stand up in front of an audience without anything to help them. There is an arsenal of tools of the trade you can consider using to make your public speaking adventure a huge success. Let's talk about each of them, how you should use them and any problems to be aware of in using those tools.

Notes

You should not feel guilty that you wish to speak from notes or even from a full script of your presentation. It is a big question that anyone who hopes to succeed in public speaking about whether to read your speech to the crowd or work from an outline. The value of the outline is that it makes you seem more relaxed and interactive with the material. The danger of an outline is that it is easy to stall out and forget what you are saying because of those sudden moments of terror that all public speakers experience on stage.

The value of reading your speech is that you know you are delivering a well prepared text and you will probably not get lost. The danger is that audiences hate to be read to and it can be a temptation to never look at them and to speak in a monotone. If you fall into that temptation, the fact that you are reading to the audience becomes such a distraction that the value of what you are saying is lost.

Handouts and Speaking Accessories

In the end, whether you read your presentation or use an outline must be a matter of personal comfort and style. Along with your notes, you also have the option of handing out notes or other support materials to help your audience stay focused. An outline of your talk with fill in blanks for the people listening to fill in can be effective. But it is not appropriate in all situations such as in a business presentation. Be aware also that anytime you give the audience something to look at, that draws attention away from you and your presentation. So use handouts with care.

Presentation Software

PowerPoint is probably the most well known presentation software and combining a PowerPoint presentation with your talk can result in a powerful experience for your audience. PowerPoint is quite easy to use and it gives you the ability to show graphs and charts, pictures, humorous examples or cartoons or even short videos to support your presentation. Here are a few tips on how to use PowerPoint effectively in your presentation.

Be absolutely certain that you will be able to use your PowerPoint presentation when you show up to give your speech. Find out if you will need to bring your own laptop and if the proper projection technology will be there and working. All it takes is one lost cable or some other missing technical link and you could lose your hard work of preparing that PowerPoint outline and be left "winging it".

Make sure the words on the screen will be easy to read by everyone in the audience. Use short phrases and a font that stands out and is easy to read. Avoid getting fancy at the expense of being understandable.

Do not put up huge blocks of text for your audience to read. They end up trying to decide whether to read your slides or listen to you.

Do not read from your PowerPoint slides to your audience. Do not stare at the screen rather than at them. Your job is talk to them not to your PowerPoint outline.

Fancy effects such as flying bullet points or cartoon characters that are easy to automate in PowerPoint are fun but distracting. Be conservative how much you use them.

Don't include too many slides. You do not want your PowerPoint slide show to dominate your public speaking moment in the sun.

Above all, if you are going to use PowerPoint to supplement your presentation, practice with the software and be very comfortable with it. Let the software become an extension of you rather than you an extension of it. If you do that and let it help you and keep the focus on what you have to say, it can be a tremendous help to you coming away from your public speaking moment with a win.

The Greatest Speaking Accessory Ever is...

The greatest speaking accessory ever is you. People will gather more information by how you look, your facial expressions and your body language than they will any other aspects of your talk. There is an old saying that goes "people hear with their eyes" and that expression is on target when it comes to public speaking.

Your presentation to that audience does not begin when you speak the first line of your prepared statements. It begins when you walk into the room. What you wear, how you greet people as you get ready to speak and even how you sit waiting to give your talk all send messages to the crowd. Then as you speak to them, your use of your body, your vocal tone and the expressions on your face tell the audience a great deal about how you feel about your subject matter.

The speakers accessories we have discussed all have value and can have a place in your presentation. But be careful how much you rely on them. It is easy for public speakers to use various helps like these to hide behind because they are nervous. Remember the presentation should always be about the subject matter. The focus should be on you and your words and the thing people should take away from your talk is a good impression of your subject matter, not of the toys you brought along with you to help you give your talk.

Chapter 11: How To Improve Your Body Language

- The first way to improve the use of body language is to watch carefully the best public speakers in the public arena or at the public speaking club to which you belong to understand how they use it effectively.

- Next, in writing your speech, look for places in the speech where your body language can enhance the speech.

- Thirdly, when you present a speech, have a friend or the club critic concentrate on looking at your use of body language, both the positive and negative aspects of it.

- Fourthly, in these days of modern technology, videotape your practice speech and then review it. Look for where you can improve and do the speech again to see how well the changes have succeeded.

- Lastly, go about your speech enthusiastically and believe in what you are saying and the 'right' body language will tend to come about automatically.

Finally, it is important to stress here that your body language is part of the whole package which is you. If you are not excited about giving a speech, your audience won't get excited either. They will see that what you are doing is not important enough for you to present it in the best possible way. Therefore, why should they get excited about it or regard it as important if you give the impression it is not?

**Gesture,
Support for a Good Speech**

Definition:

Gesture is the movement of the body, head, arms and hands, together with facial expressions, to add emphasis and greater meaning to an idea or an emotion during an oral presentation or speech. It helps make a well written and researched speech into a better spoken presentation.

The Do's of Gesture:

Below are some startling points you might consider to allow you to add gesture to your oral presentations.

- Before you start to speak and/or gesture, have a neutral starting position - a stance without a gesture. This will give greater impact to your gesture.

- You must now let your hands be your friends when speaking. Don't leave them hanging at your side.

- Your gesture must be relevant to what you say.

- Use gesture to demonstrate or stress the idea/s you are suggesting.

- Gesture from the shoulder, not just the hands or wrists or from the elbow.

- Make your gestures a whole body experience.

- Your gestures must be expansive. Make sure you spread out your fingers to induce the expansiveness. (Watching singing groups like The Drifters, you will see the expansive use of the hands, fingers and arms to enhance their performance).

- Leaning forward towards your audience at appropriate times in your speech can make the audience feel more included in what you are saying.

- When you want to gesture, the brain, the voice and the body must be in tune with each other.

- Learn to 'relax' your body. Nervousness curtails the impact of good gesture. Remember the audience is on your side. They want you to give a great speech.

- After you have written and practiced your speech, plan where and what sort of gesture you will use. Often, the gesture will just occur naturally through the emotion of your words as you practice.

- When you have decided where and what gestures you will use, print out your speech double spaced so that you can mark, in a different colour, where and what gesture you will use. This will help you if you have a lectern and intend to use your written notes to deliver your speech.

- You may need to use variations in pitch, loudness and the speed of your words to fit in with your gesture and the impact you want to produce in your audience.

- Your body language must compliment your gesture, e.g. a smile may not go with a serious point you are making.

The Don'ts of Gesture:

- Don't shuffle, sway, or pace up and down and don't be immobile. These body movements will cause a loss of the visual impact that your gesture can add to your words.

- It is important to ensure you do not have automatic gestures (mannerisms) that detract from what you are saying, i.e. meaningless and repetitive gestures. The Prime Minister, Mr. Tony Abbot, is an example of a public speaker who often uses repetitive gestures that don't seem to support what he is saying). A neutral standing position will have less negative impact on the message of your speech than gesture that is not related to the theme of the speech.

When to gesture:

- Look for words in your speech that could indicate to you an action e. g. in a speech "Flying High" I wrote and performed, there was scope to use my arms to indicate an eagle flying high or swooping down in a dive.

- Double space the printing of your speech and go through it indicating words or phrases that imply the need for gesture.
- Decide on what sort of gesture to use in each spot.
- Practise the gesture only after you have mastered the words of your speech.
- In your conclusion, you could use the same gesture you used before in your speech to emphaise a point made earlier.

Remember that good gesture can add greater meaning and appeal to your speech. However, this can only truly happen if your speech is a good product. Great gesture will not rescue a poor speech.

Just as writing a good speech is always a work in progress, so is creating the best gesture to go with each new speech you deliver. So, continue to watch how the best speakers you know use gesture. Then, when you see something new, note it and find a place to use it in a future speech thus continuing your development as a speaker.

Chapter 12: Visual Aid Activity

Ibrahim Abou Ghalioum

Topic: This activity teaches students the differences between a good visual aid and a bad visual aid, as well as how to work in a small to medium sized group to quickly develop a presentation.

Learning Objectives: This learning activity is designed to:

- Promote practical application of effective visual aid construction by critiquing/revising a poorly constructed visual aid

- Promote effective group communication to create an effective visual aid

Description of Assignment/Activity: Students break up into groups and each group gets a paper with a visual aid on it (typically a slide from a PowerPoint) that does a poor job in terms of style, content, or both. They must then construct a new visual aid that does the job properly.

Materials needed: Each group must have at least 1 person with a laptop/tablet with PowerPoint access.

Prep time: 30-45 minutes of online research to find the visual aids that students will be improving. Each group should have a different visual aid that they will be improving. Be sure to create a "presentation" so that the entire class can see the "bad" examples during the debrief.

Assignment time: 50 minutes - 1 hour

Instructions for Instructor:

1. Decide how many groups you will break your students into, and then find examples of poor visual aids on the internet and print them out so that each group will get one.

2. Notify your students beforehand to bring their laptops to class that day.

Instructions for Students:

1. Break into groups (# of students per group will vary based on class size. 3-4 works well for this activity)

2. Discuss for approx. 10-15 minutes what is wrong with the visual aid I give you. Look at the color scheme, the font, the background, etc. Also look at the content - Does it make sense? Are there misleading charts/graphs? Is there too much text? Is the source of the data properly cited? Apply everything you've learned about effective visual aids.

3. For the next 10-15 minutes, design an alternative to the slide on one group member's laptop, where you fix the problems mentioned in #2. Your revised slide must be emailed to me at the end of learning activity for class display.

4. Each group will perform a 2-3 minute presentation (all group members must speak). I will show the "bad" visual to the class while your group identifies

the opportunities for improvement and how they were addressed in the new version.

5. After you present, we will open class discussion to evaluate your newly constructed visual to make sure it is effective.

Necessary Background: This should be given sometime before a speech requiring visual aids, after you have already presented content on slideshow presentations and visual aids.

Special considerations: You need a technology-enabled classroom to display the visual aids.

Debrief: Go over the differences between bad visual aids and good visual aids, recalling points you mentioned in earlier lessons, as well as recalling good points that students made during their speeches for the activity.

Variations: Using visual aids from the classroom (ex: laptop cases, business cards, baseball caps)

Trouble spots: Students miss what some of the weaknesses are in the visual aids given to them. These should be mentioned at the end of the speech in a positive way ("good job students, let's take another look at…"). You can also open this discussion up to the class ("What else needs to be considered regarding the effectiveness of this visual aid?")

Common questions students ask:

- Does our speech need an intro and conclusion? Org. structure? Answer: Yes.

- Can the new slide we create look totally different than the old one? Answer: Yes.

- Should we find a chart/graph online or create a new one ourselves if we want to replace a misleading chart/graph on our old visual aid? Answer: Entirely up to you.

Chapter 13: What Qualities Do You Need?

For communication to be effective, the attention of your audience hooked to your every word and inspiring them simultaneously is a task on its own and for you to achieve this, you will be required to be an effective speaker. The encoding and relay of the message has to be accurate for the reception to be good.

Here are some of the qualities you will need to develop in order to succeed:

- *Confidence:* Here it comes again. Confidence proves to be one of the most important components in this field.

A study was published by University of Wolverhampton which stated that: "A highly confident speaker is viewed as being more accurate, competent, credible, intelligent, knowledgeable, likable, and believable than less confident uncertain speaker."

This gives you an idea of how important it is to develop your confidence.

- *Be Yourself:* It is importance to be natural and yourself when you are on stage and presenting. You need to practice and be prepared with what you want to say but try not to memorize the speech. It should come naturally to you. Memorizing might just make to fumble and stammer if you forget any part of the presentation. So make sure you are knowledgeable about the subject you are going to speak on.

- *Passion:* Your passion for the subject you are presenting will help inspire the audience and you cannot fake that. You have to find your interest because without that your speech will lack the spark your audience will be looking for.

- *Natural with modulation:* You cannot make your voice perfect; it will end up sounding fake. And you will eventually lose your audience. Use your natural voice with a conversational tone and that will keep it authentic. But there is need of voice modulations to keep the piece interesting. Modulations in the voice will break the monotonous flow of a rehearsed speech. If your audience starts to feel that you have memorized the speech and delivering, they will lose interest.

- *Short and Simple:* Dragging is boring. Just because you have been allotted an hour doesn't mean you have to keep talking for the entire time. You don't want your audience to sleep off. So keep it to the point. Once you have put your point forward and the presentation is done, open the floor for questions or feedback. There is no harm in letting your audience go a little early.

- *Repetition, Summarize and Conclude:* It will be great if you can emphasize on the main points a couple of times just ensure that the audience are definitely taking away the main point. Also a good practice would be to summarize effective at the end of the session to ensure that audience doesn't miss out on any point and any misunderstanding might be clarified during the summarization and conclusion parts.

Chapter 14: Principles Of Public Speaking

Here are a few principles of which a public speaker should be mindful.

1. Breathing

Correct breathing is extremely important for a speaker
· Practice breathing through your nose
· Breathe deeply right to the bottom of your lungs
· Practice filling your chest and lungs with air
· Hold the air in your lungs and breath out slowly
· Let the air come right up from the bottom of your lungs through larynx (voice box) and hit the roof of your mouth. The roof of your mouth should act as a sounding board. When you bounce your voice off your palate, it will gain extra resonance and will strengthen your vocal chords.

2. Articulation

Articulation is the art of uttering speech clearly. An articulate person speaks very clearly and he is easy to understand, because he pronounces his words well. Every speaker should aim to become adept in this skill. He ought to be easy to listen to. It should not impose strain to listen to you as a speaker; it should be pleasure. Practice speaking clearly even in everyday conversation.

3. Inflection

Inflection in speech has to do with the pitch of your voice. The human voice has a very wide range of tones. If you speak at same pitch and on the same tone all the time, your voice can sound very boring. You must develop the ability to modulate your voice.

As a singer can go up and down the scale –giving forth a good variety of tones –so can the public speaker. If your voice is naturally high-pitched, you must practice speaking in the lower registers. Develop a variety of pitch in your voice.

4. Speed of Delivery

Speed of delivery has to do with the rate at which you speak. Some people tend to speak at the same rate all the time. This can become rather boring and a burden to listen to such people for long.

You should endeavour to vary the speed at which you speak. Most of your speech should be delivered at a moderate rate, which is easy to listen to. From time to time, however, you should quicken or slow down the pace to give variety and added emphasis to your presentation.

5. Volume

This is another factor of great importance when it comes to public speaking. Varying the volume of your voice can give added emphasis to a point you wish to make. The major part of your message should be delivered at a conversational volume. This ensures that it is loud enough for all to hear, yet not so loud, that it assaults the ears of the audience.

Some Speakers seem to feel it necessary to speak so loud that they hurt the ears of their hearers. Try to avoid this. Endeavour to begin your speaking at conversational volume and turn the volume right up when you have a special point to emphasize strongly. If you occasionally drop the volume, this will also serve to give special emphasis and draw attention of the audience to hang on to every word you speak.

6. Pausing

Don't be afraid to pause once in a while. This can also give added emphasis to some point you make. Some speakers are frightened of quiet spots and therefore make their delivery pour forth like a torrential rain without any pause making it difficult for the audience to absorb.

Your audience needs time to think and consider what you have said so that they can truly absorb the truth of your message. You need to inform the mind as well as stir the emotions. The mind can absorb things only at a study rate. If you speak too fast without suitable pauses, you will leave your audience behind.

7. Repetition

A certain amount of repetition is necessary in public speaking as it helps emphasize your point and fix it in the minds of your audience.

Try to present the same point in a variety of ways so that the idea or truth you are sharing will become part of the thinking and action of the audience.

In order to achieve this however, the mind needs an adequate exposure of truth and must be convinced to do so through the conscious and the purposeful repetition of that truth.

Chapter 15: How To Find A Topic Or A Subject To Talk About

Here, you will discover the three factors that make that exercise possible. It is a conscious and active exercise of your mind you need to get involved in.

You are seating at a table, in a restaurant with a group of people waiting for their food. Everybody is silent. And all of the sudden someone strikes a topic, and everyone is so interested, everyone is voicing their own opinion, things are getting even more interesting, with jokes and laughter. What happened? How did he or she do that? There are three main factors to consider. The **people** around you, the **place** you are at and the **circumstances** you are in.

People. If you want to find conversation topic easily, you need to consider your audience or the people around you. Have an idea about their interests, their tendencies, their taste, their aspirations, their passion, their work, their family, their health etc. So being able to start a conversation in their field of interest. The best way to start is to ask a question. For example, you want to start a conversation at a table, and your direct interlocutor is a lawyer, and you would say for instance, " Sir what you think of that famous journalist murder case? If your interlocutor was a crèche owner, you would ask for an example. Mrs x, how do you manage that big number of children coming to your crèche this year? and so forth.

The **place**. Here it is important to know that some topics are totally irrelevant in some places. For example, at a funeral, most of the attention is focused on the deceased and the conversions would mostly funeral related. So you will need to study the place or environment before starting a topic of conversation. Different places require different conversational approach. So please as you all are standing in the churchyard and waiting for the service to begin, Don't ask " sir can you please tell me the name of your favourite porn star? " if you do, make sure your mum didn't hear you. Why? Because it is irrelevant and inappropriate.

The **circumstances**. Here we have two aspects. Our conversation with others and the fortuitous events that unfold during the conversation. Our convention with other is like a game. It is not difficult to find a topic. Someone has just said something interesting and not necessarily a question. Your duty is to kind of " keep the fire burning", by reformulating the same thing in a more stimulating and interesting way. You can add something extra, add examples that are related to the topic, give your personal interpretation etc, that is how you get to introduce a discussion or conversation just based on a simple line you managed to keep alive through your ingenuity. The **fortuitous events that occur during the conversation.** These are unpredictable, they could be remarks, a simple question raised by a colleague or someone sitting at the table. In this case, you need to be yourself and try to be more alert and spontaneous regarding what everyone says. Your good sense of humour, as well as your unique personality, can cause a great ambience for everybody to be interested in sharing their opinions even the most silent guest. *To find a topic or a subject for a conversation is essential, to find out what your audience interests are* *and using your own imagination, topped with your personality and sense of humour come up with the relevant line.*

Chapter 16: Everybody Has A Different Perspective

My high school teaching life certainly didn't last long. The vagaries of teacher shortages at the time meant there were few permanent positions on offer and contracts tended to occur through networks or to those with surnames beginning with the letters A-S. Only fellow S-Z's will understand.

Side note: I have always been a "W" - both with my married and single surnames. I often considered the benefits of creating a class action on "alphabetism". Unless your surname starts with any letter further up the alphabet than "S" you can't join the litigation process. Across my whole life, school, childhood immunisation (before disposable needles - you'll need to think it through to understand the ramifications), in graduation classes and various employers, virtually any list I'm on anywhere is approached alphabetically. The consequences are that those of us at the end of the line miss out on stuff - applications, phone calls, prizes, special events and more. The problem is who to sue? Everybody with a surname starting with A to R? I'm still thinking on it.

After less than a year of teaching I discovered that teenagers were more aggressive than I remember from my era: demanding, loud, unpredictable and generally a 'challenge'. My last day teaching in a high school involved a student who locked herself in a room as a joke, banged on the window resulting in a glass-embedded arm and a trip to emergency – for me not her.

At the time there was a glut of teachers and few permanent teaching places available - coinciding with a surge in unemployment generally. My chances of a permanent teaching position were slim, even though I had graduated with the top 'Suitability Rating'.

About the time the shattered window matched my confidence I was offered a role teaching the long-term unemployed. To say I jumped at the opportunity to teach adults would be a fairly literal description. Further to my previous observations, teenagers' preoccupation with interests other than school fell into reasonably distinct groups.

Grade 8 – still young enough to be quietened by a stern look, they are into toilet humour but quickly discovering independence not available to them in primary school and testing boundaries with adults is viewed as a legitimate sport. However, if you don't embarrass Grade 8's with too much attention they can still be great fun.

Grade 9 – they now know at least enough about sex to find anything sounding remotely like a sexual word to be highly amusing and they are quickly adapting to the realisation that teachers have little real power to control them. Asking them to do anything can result in threats of lawsuits and harassment claims.

Grade 10 – know more about sex and if they aren't 'doing it' (or pretending they are) know 'like' someone who is and 'like' can't see the point in school. Teachers, parents and adults generally are 'like' basically 'like' idiots. Eye rolling is an art form.

Grade 11 – if they aren't 'doing it' they have a good reason and will give you their opinion on anything and everything whether you want to hear it or not. They have strong political, social, environmental and other opinions that are based on, well, not much.

Grade 12 – it is assumed they are all 'doing it' and romance is everywhere but it is uncool (or whatever the latest word is) to talk about it as it is nobody's business and they are too busy working or studying and just want to finish with high school. If you can get their trust the teaching experience can be very rewarding.

This may have changed since I was teaching and I am happy to be corrected. Smart phones are new but not the smart attitude. And before you tweet me that I have over-generalised – don't bother, I know I have. I have met and know many wonderful, well-adjusted and frighteningly mature teenagers but they can be formidable as a cohort.

Besides, teenagers throw things, only value their own opinions, have shifting allegiances, and they smell. I hadn't really enjoyed high school teaching as much as I had imagined I would. The prospect of a class of adults was truly inviting.

Some people of my acquaintance thought I was crazy taking on this new role. The long-term unemployed don't usually get great press and have a general reputation for not wanting to work.

It is true that adult classes are unlikely to threaten legal action if you ask them to actually do something and there are fewer odour issues (theirs not mine). Adult males are also less inclined to show off in front of females – ok, it's a bit more subtle. However, I soon discovered that anyone forced to attend a class to get welfare payment or a pass mark or being compliant with some government or organisational requirement makes a less than receptive student.

Sadly too, some adults can be just as obstructive, destructive, counterproductive and surprisingly influenced by others just like high school students – it is just quieter.

Back to my first adults only teaching experience - I had been employed to deliver Certificates III and IV in Business Administration to groups of ten long-term unemployed individuals who were made to attend the course to meet new criteria for continued receipt of welfare payments. My first day was nerve-wracking. I was making it up on the fly as there were no course materials, no guidelines and no supervision. Starting from scratch on an eight-week course I was drawing on resources I had collected over the years and, as mentioned, generally making it up. This was during the very early days of the Internet where there wasn't really much to search for. Now there are whole courses ready for download — cheating really.

Side note: This will come as a surprise to many but some trainers (at least those who can cope with it) are sometimes only one page ahead of their students. In fact, the trick with software training when it all goes to hell is to ask the student group to problem solve, "How would you fix it?" while you unobtrusively but frantically check the manual for an answer.

I can't really recall the profile of the class but suffice to say they had been unemployed for a minimum of two years – the criteria for being able to attend these classes.

The first day of the course set the scene for an incredible learning curve (for me not them). Lesson plan in hand I followed the correct AQF guidelines (Australian Qualifications Framework) on outlining the course and its learning outcomes and launched into delivering the content of the first subject.

I began the day covering the outline, learning outcomes and general content they would expect to cover over the next eight weeks, fire escapes, breaks, housekeeping blah, blah, blah. You know, the usual stuff you have to do but to which few people are listening.

(Having said that, I have discovered over the years there are usually one or two in the group who will obsess about process and will not hesitate to tell you that sections of your outline were not covered, there were spelling mistakes, where the workbook doesn't match the slides, you didn't do an evacuation drill, breaks, and so on). Controlling eye roll can be difficult in these situations.

The air-conditioned room was tranquil and serene. Ten faces look towards me, hanging on every word. Lovely. No answering back, no 'Miss, he spat at me'. Joyful attention from all students in the room. Apparently.

After the morning break the class resumed with a noticeable absentee. My small class of ten had become nine. On enquiry it transpired that the student wasn't detained or otherwise engaged, she had left the building with no plans to return. Apparently her need to escape the classroom with alacrity was a result of my opening statements where I had tapped into her greatest fear. Really? Please explain?

"You said there would be an assignment to be completed by the end of the course." "In fact, some of us are still considering whether we come back tomorrow."

The missing student was clearly allergic to the idea of being assessed and had hightailed out of the building at the first opportunity – never to return.

Well then. Let's move on.

Testing had, for many in the room, been the cause of failure, humiliation and regret. Schooling for the most part had not been a happy experience. No one can say I'm a slow learner. From that day forward and for the following four years of teaching that course and others I left the "A" word entirely out of any conversation until week three of the program. By this stage I was either a friend, a mother figure, or they just liked me enough to want to prove to me that they could, and would, complete the task. I didn't lose another student in the following four years – except if they got work (which they frequently did). Bonus.

At the time, the government of the day was only funding skills development for the very long-term unemployed - perhaps the unemployable. Surprisingly, the four years I spent teaching business skills to individuals who had been out of paid work for between two and 20 years turned out to be the most enlightening of my career. Officially the course was Certificate IV Business Administration. However, I quickly discovered that to successfully complete the eight week business course I needed to set the scene for each new group with the non-accredited module: Workplace Basics 101.

This module covered the following non-accredited but incredibly under-rated expectations and requirements:

- Turn up on time and stay all day - it is doable.
- A 9am doctor's appointment does not mean you take the whole day off.
- When the computer screen shows stars or goes blank it doesn't mean you've broken it.
- Learning can be fun and rewarding.
- Once they were competent in the Basics we progressed to Business Ownership 101:
- Businesses that make money hire more people.
- Profit and cash are not the same thing.
- No-one HAS to employ you.
- Wages are not the only employee costs.

And finally graduating with the Module:

- You really can speak in Public and not Die.

All delivered without PowerPoint (amazing isn't it?).

What I learned over those intense four years was humbling. My understanding of the long- term unemployed was misguided and I discovered some commonalities in my classrooms. These observations of the unemployed were some years ago and the world have moved on and I wonder if much has changed.

They moved a lot – making it difficult for government agencies, potential employers, superannuation, insurance and other important correspondence to find them.

They had an unrealistic view of what 'business' and 'work' was – business people get to keep all the money they make apparently (paying no taxes, bills, Work cover, insurance, etc.). Getting paid large wages and rapid promotion was a right rather than something you had to work for necessarily, if you didn't feel like it today.

They loved drama – life was boring if there were no family disputes, broken hearts or feuding neighbours. Television shows with high drama were often a lunchtime talking point.

The level of education was not necessarily an indicator of limited employment opportunities. Most students had finished high school and many students had certificates, degrees, and even the occasional masters. What they didn't have was personal or career goals (except for winning lotto). They just wanted a job. Defining what that job might look like was far less clear. I recall asking one student in her mid-twenties who had a degree in multi-media and another in communication what job she was looking for. "Something in media." What a great goal. "Which field of media are you interested in?" She could only reply 'anything in media'. Print, film, television? No amount of probing could elicit further clarification of her dream job.

Strippers, refugees, battered women, car accident victims, bullies, recovering drug addicts, ex-cons, new widows, those recovering from debilitating illnesses and assorted bad luck stories allowed me to connect with them to learn more, discover themselves and blossom.

It is a time I cherish. Before that experience I was not aware of just how fortunate I had been to have love, trust, consistency and hope as the basis of my relationships with family and friends.

Note to self: No matter how much you think you know other people know stuff you don't know. Just because you are up the front of the room doesn't mean you shouldn't be humble.

Everybody views the world differently. We all have experiences and histories which make us very diverse. While I'd be lying if I said I don't judge others, I do. However, I try to temper my judgement by endeavouring to view the world as they might - listen and learn. I'm not perfect and neither are they.

Standing up the front pontificating is the easy bit, remaining humble is the harder skill — many people in the room may know more than you or might be insulted, challenged, or worse bored by you or what you are saying.

Probably my greatest joy from that time was being able to contribute to the personal and professional growth of individuals, who despite a range of misfortunes (some self-inflicted), wanted to be appreciated and given the skills and an opportunity to succeed. Every group and all students taught me something about myself and the world outside my privileged bubble.

Flexibility is the key to winning an audience's trust and engagement. Each group of delegates has a collective 'personality'. Tapping into that personality early, adjusting to their requirements will win hearts and minds. Check their knowledge level as best you can, when you can. When you only have a one-off and short opportunity to engage and inform this is clearly a challenge.

Body language is often your only 'tell' that you are missing the mark. Multiple eyes down furtively texting is a reasonably good indicator - though it could be just rudeness or urgent response required to someone's picture of last night's dinner.

Lesson 5 – Risk manage your talk by conceding (at least in your head, if not publically), that some in the audience will know part, others everything about your topic and acknowledge that your talk may only consolidate rather than illuminate. Each delegate will have different experiences, a different learning style, state of mind, pressures and stresses which will affect how they listen to and interpret your message.

Chapter 17: ◊ Spirit & Source

Platform speaking: a public Rorschach test.
 Jack's New Edge Dictionary

Any kind of *performance,* especially public speaking, is a *high spiritual experience* and a graphic metaphor for our lives. Let me say this emphatically: There is nothing more spiritual than public speaking and performance. Performance *mythologizes*. Performance *exaggerates*. Whatever is hidden *demands to be released*. Anything that sits in *denial* demands its day on stage. Sure, we can continue to hide behind walls of old protection, but as we desire expanded venue for ourselves, these fear-based beliefs, patterns and protections must be encountered.

Your *intention* is as important to your performance results as any other part of the game. What is your intention when it comes to the audience? What is your intention for the speech/performance? What outcome do you want?

To create an atmosphere of communion with an audience, your *intention is paramount*.

You see, *audience* and *performer wants the same thing, a magic experience*. This magic only happens in the present moment. And the present moment is only available if the speaker or performer has cleared all the junk and bunk and funky residue out of his/her comfort zone.

Source

I call my work SourceWork. The implication is that at the source of our beings we are *powerful, creative, brave, present* and *whole*. In the process of growing up, birth trauma, Mommy,

Daddy, Uncle Harry, Sister Regina and society in general have greatly contributed to the muffling of these great potentials.

To tap into that wellspring of power and inspiration, we must clear our conduits of expression. In other words, anything that blocks this power must be dealt with, or we're not really free to express. Remember, an audience shows up to get an *experience of you*. Your subject may lure us in, but what we want is an experience of you. Your job is to break down the walls and give us more and more of you. *Tune into the source* of your being, *express from that source* and *cycle the energy* of the audience. This is the most important secret of speaking and performance.

Channeling energy

When it comes to speaking and performance, the audience may say they want information, data, entertainment, and overtly, they do. But they want it delivered in an energy

sandwich. It's the *exchange of energy* they're after. They want inspiration, and they can't get it *unless you're inspired*. More to the point: *you won't be inspired unless you're channeling the audience's energy*.
Communion.

Afraid they'll lose their train of thought, too many speakers and performers keep the audience out. The opposite is glaring and true. By surrendering to and merging with your audience, you get to use the energy of the audience and ride it like a zephyr.
Communion.

The audience can be trusted to give energy, not the focus. You provide that. You're the focus (and sometimes the filter) for the energy and the expectation of the audience.
Communion.

It may be you talking, but it's us speaking
Communion.

Holy Trio

CONTENT

CONNECTION COMFORT

This is the Holy Trio of performance:

CONTENT: *Have a good grasp on your material.* Know your subject, script, speech.

CONNECTION: *Breathe the audience in.* Most novice speakers and performers do just the opposite. They are so concerned about being perfect and delivering their material flawlessly that they keep the audience out, thereby isolating themselves and eliminating the possibility of accessing the audience energy.

COMFORT: *Surf the present moment.* Of course, if your comfort zone is rigid and tight, being in the present moment is all-but-impossible. ANYTHING THAT KEEPS YOU OUT OF THE PRESENT DESTROYS COMMUNION! (I could have called this last leg Presence, but then it wouldn't begin with a "C", now would it?)

Another way of saying this: if you have a good grasp on your material, you can relax into the present moment, embrace the audience and its energy and take us on a memorable ride!

> *Jack'S TiDBIT:*
> **The Centering Breath: Before you begin**

> **speaking — to any audience, for any reason — take a big, slow breath and breathe us in. Take in the audience energy, don't keep us out.**

Be Here Now

"BE HERE NOW"
One of the first new age books, written by Ram Das in the late 1960's

As far as I'm concerned, we could have eliminated the new age entirely if we would have just grasped the title to Ram Das's book. The *present moment* is the entire podium for action in speaking and performance. You can rehearse till you can say your lines backwards in your sleep. You can practice gestures and mannerisms till you look like a third base coach. You can modulate your voice like Richard Burton on acid. We're still not going to be touched unless you jump into the present moment with us.

Technique is great, technique is grand, technique is ever-so-lovely, but let me say this ad nauseam: what the audience is after is an *experience of you*. In a day where way too many speech teachers are putting the technique horse before the source cart, I can't over-emphasize the value of making a real connection with your audience, and trusting the miracle of present time.

Highest possibility for performance

Shamanic healing: the shaman merges with the subject and heals himself.
 The Way of the Hawk

Speaker healing: the speaker merges with the audience and heals everybody.

Jack's New Edge Dictionary

Public performance is a privilege. When one truly considers the transformational potential in performance, it's not so unusual that speaking is our biggest fear. Let me state it definitively. The highest possibility for a speech or a performance of any kind is to *inspire us*, to *provoke us*, to *lead us to great heights*.

Communion.

> *Jack'S TiDBIT:*
> **If you want to read a current book about the**

> **present, try** The Power of Now **by Ekhart Tolle.**

The Two Kinds of Jokes You Should Never Tell

Humor is such a vital ingredient to a great speech, yet it is somehow overlooked on a regular basis. Don't do this. Failure to use humor in a speech is almost an inconsiderate thing to do to your audience. When you perform humor in front of a crowd, it lets them know that you are keeping them in the front of your mind. There are many other reasons why you should do this, including making them feel more relaxed and giving yourself a sense of likability.

However, there are two kinds of jokes that I never, ever wish to hear you joke about (unless you really, really, really, and I mean really, know what you're doing).

The first kind of joke you should never tell an audience is a joke about 9/11. Please, for the love of religious figures, just avoid any jokes about collapsing buildings, airplanes, or any event in which a lot of people died in a very short period of time. While there certainly does exist a population of people who would probably laugh at those kinds of jokes, it's better to stay on the safe side and not make them. Unless you are a famous, well-known, well-paid professional such as the comedian Gilbert Gottfried, any jokes about 9/11 are inevitably bound to work against you during your speech.

The second kind of joke that you should try to avoid altogether are jokes that are racist in nature. Unless it is already expected of you by the audience before your speech, then just don't bother to tell them. The thing is, that even if the joke were truly funny and even done in a tasteful manner, chances are that people would be too afraid to laugh out loud because they would be worried at what the person sitting next to them would think of them.

Both of these are extremely risky maneuvers that provide little reward even if you do succeed with the joke. Even though I highly suggest that these should almost never be made to an audience, it doesn't mean that there are limits to public speaking.

A secret that I've learned with public speaking is that if a speaker is good enough, is trained well enough, and is experienced enough, he or she can get away with saying anything in front of an audience. Of course, this is also dependent upon how well the speaker supports his or her idea or comment with a sound discourse.

As far as content in a speech goes, I am not here to tell you about how to construct your speech. I'm just here to address the fear of public speaking and how to create an enticing, interesting presence on stage by controlling your physical body.

What I will tell you, is that assuming you are at least somewhat decent in constructing a logical argument of some sort, then there are no limits to what you can say to an audience if you have an awesome stage presence.

If you are confused by what I am talking about, then allow me to demonstrate that concept with this example.

There once was a man named Adolf Hitler who convinced millions of people in Germany to do his bidding, and believe just about anything he said. He almost single-handedly caused several countries to take sides and fight against each other.

Was Hitler born into a wealthy family? No. was Hitler born into a family with strong political connections? No. Did he even have any highly distinguishing merits before he came to power? Not really. So how did Hitler acquire so much popularity and control over Germany in a relatively short period of time?

The answer was that he was a great public speaker. Hitler would study American sportscasters that would energize a crowd of spectators into a frenzy during football games, and borrowed techniques used by these sportscasters to rile the German people. Let Hitler's actions in the past serve as a reminder of the true power of public speaking, which can be used for either good or bad. Realize that although it was unfortunate that he used his power in a way that many consider destructive, there is nothing that can really stop you from achieving your purpose in a public speech. Whether you want to persuade an audience to change their opinion on an issue, or teach them something, there is almost no limit as to what you can convince an audience to do as long as you use the tools at your disposal well enough.

How's this for a secret that you probably won't find in most public speaking books?

Chapter 18: How To Deliver Speech

Monore's motivational sequence

Giving your public speech is always a new experience whether you are delivering it for the first time or you are an experienced speaker. The reason behind this is because every time when you start delivering your speech, you have to face a new audience in different circumstances & with a different way of approach. Whatever be the circumstances or the subject of the presentation, you should always follow a universal sequence of delivering your speech. This type of universal sequence is known as Monore's motivational sequence. According to this, the speaker must involve themselves into a series of sequences with the audience to deliver an effective speech. These sequences are:
☐ **Attention**
☐ **Need**

- ☐ **Satisfaction**
- ☐ **Visualization**
- ☐ **Action**

Attention

The first & foremost thing for an effective speech is to grab the attention of the audience by the speaker. To do this, you can start your speech with a story, predictions, shocking statistics, photos, videos etc.

Need

Once you have got the attention, it's time now to show that the topic of your speech is relevant to them. Let them convince that they should not avoid listening to your topic.

Satisfaction

In this stage, your duty is to present the solutions of the stated problems in your speech. Your statement of approach should be specific, clear, straight & also must be well understandable by the audience. Give your best to convince them that your approach of solving the situation is one of the best & also well efficient. You can use practical examples or own experiences to make the solutions more convincing.

Visualization

In this step, your task is to tell the audience about the final result of the solutions given by you & what will be happened if they stick to your ideas. In this context, there are two methods related to this. If you are considering the method of telling the audience with the benefits of following something, this is called the Positive method. While, if you are providing the factors for not following it, it is referred as negative method. You can use any one of these methods in your speech or presentation. Better way is to compare both the positive & negative aspects & convince them the benefits of one method.

Action

The final step of Monore's sequence method is the action taken by the audience with respect to the solutions you have stated in your speech. Make a brief yet powerful final statement which convinces them to follow your solutions.

Factors that keep in mind during presentation

Pronunciation

Most of the speakers are unable to reach the audience or unable to grab audience attention is because of the lack of clear pronunciation of the tricky yet useful words. Give your time to pronounce each & every word of your speech clearly & slowly. Try to avoid the use of complicated words instead.

Anxiety control

Almost all the presenter feels at least minimum anxiety before their speech. Anxiety can be reduced with the increase in self-confidence & with good knowledge about the topic. Also, just before the speech, take few seconds to organize yourself in front of the audience. Taking a deep breath before the speech is much beneficial.

First impression

The first impression makes the base for your entire presentation or speech. You should dress appropriately with neat, clean cloths & also should be comfortable enough to make your gestures accurately.

Postures

Good postures are very essential for an effective speech or presentation. You should stand straight with your face towards the audience. Your body weight should eventually distribute throughout the time on the stage.

Gestures

Positive gestures significantly increase your self-confidence during the time on the stage. When you feel discomfort or awkward during your speech, make some slow movements like: walking a few steps on the stage & make yourself relax.

Eye contact

Eye contact with the audience is one of the ways to calm yourself during your speech. Try to have eye contact with a person from the audience from the very beginning. Do speak to that person until you make a connection with them. As you get that person's attention, move to a different person & so on. Eye contact with the people helps to maintain the audience interest throughout the time of your speech.

Avoid reading

Avoid reading only from the slides or from any visual aids you are using in your presentation or speech. You should use it as a supplementary to your concept not for read out purpose.

Facial expressions

Show your good & positive feelings towards the topic of your speech or presentation. This is one of the must need tools for a good speech.

Avoid filler words

Filler words like 'um', 'ah', 'you know' should be avoided during the speech.

Instead, you can maintain silence during the rehearsal of your speech before the stage presentation & try to lessen it with more practicing session. This will be helpful to avoid filler words completely during final stage presentation.

Rehearsal

Practice makes one perfect. Practice your speech or presentation again & again. You can do it in front of your friends or silently in your head. Ask your friends to give feedback & ask them to point out in which areas you have to work more. A complete dress rehearsal is equally important before the final presentation.

Chapter 19: Feedback

Feedback as much as you are practicing and delivering real speeches in front of a real audience getting, feedback from people that you trust is a great way to continue to improve your speaking skills and notably how you are doing from a fear stage fear perspective. Feedback is a powerful mechanism powerful mechanism and you can get feedback from anybody. But then if you only want to get feedback from people that you trust that is fine too. Now as many validations as possible. I'm not talking about feedback in a home setting in the privacy of your home or any simulated setting.

You need real feedback.

When you were talking in front of a real audience for real speech the reason I say that is because in a home setting you are not being able to generate all the different conditions that come together which will otherwise happen in a real setting. You don't have all the people you don't have the typical stage we're in a home setting. So once you go on stage in a real setting real audience real conference room real seminar hall the variables the factors are very different. So having somebody who will say hey this is how we are dead and offer you critical feedback constructively.

Could be good feedback is key.

Now what you thought are your problems may not even be your problems. They may not even be problems that could be entirely different ones. You might be thinking your hands are trembling but then the person sitting in the audience may not even have notice that they must have noticed something else completely different. So what your thought of your problems may not be a problem that could be completely new ones or on the good side.

There may not be any problems so many of these problems might simply be residing in your head. So getting that feedback from any number of people from any number of real speeches is key but what is also key is being receptive to feedback because as much as we say oh I am trying to get feedback. Most of us are not receptive to getting real constructively critical feedback.

So being open to that and being open to work the feedback into your Makes speech and make continual improvements. Is fundamental to becoming a great speaker and fundamental to conquering your fear of public speaking. The feedback is key.

Bullet

The silver bullet the question is Is there a silver bullet to conquer your stage fear something that you can do. Magically that will take away all your fear of public speaking. If you ask me, The answer is a big yes absolutely. There is a silver bullet and it is not what you think it is not a magic pill it's not a red pill blue pill solution. It is simply one of speaking in as many real events as possible and that is the key to real events. Now you can speak a hundred times at home you can speak a hundred times in front of a minute but nothing compares to being in front of a real audience and giving a real speech.

By the way I don't approve of speaking in front of a mirror that has no practical use as much as you think it is. That is so speaking at home or speaking in the close confines of your office other safe spaces. It's not going to help as much. I mean you can practice. Certainly that is the way to practice but getting over the fear will call for standing in front of a real audience and delivering a real speech. And the more you do it the faster you can get over the fear of public speaking. The initial jitteriness that comes upon any speaker no matter how experienced you are so go speak and there are any number of forums where you can give real speeches.

One that comes to mind is Toastmasters. There are many many people trying to get over the fear of public speaking. So become a member of a Toastmasters club that is closest to you. Maybe your organization has one or call for a brown bag every Friday in your office and create an opportunity to speak so the more you speak the more you are in front of a real audience. The sooner you are going to get over the fear of speaking get over the initial anxiety.

So practice is great. But speaking in real events that is the magic trick.

Chapter 20: Make Your Talk Interesting

> *"They may forget what you said, but they will never forget how you made them feel."*

Communication is not just verbal. Many people believe this to be true. In fact, as written on finance.yahoo.com, *"only a small percentage of communication involves actual words: 7%, to be exact. In fact, 55% of communication is visual (body language, eye contact) and 38% is vocal (pitch, speed, volume, tone of voice). The world's best business communicators have strong body language: a commanding presence that reflects confidence, competence, and charisma."* This is so important to know. It's the reason why it is so important that once you create your talk, you practice, practice, practice.

You are going to see me talk about practicing a lot, because when all is said and done, it's the one who practices who keeps the job and/or makes the most money. Remember this.

I love this quote by Brian Tracy, *"Practice is the price of mastery. Whatever you practice over and over again becomes a new habit of thought and performance."*

So outside of practicing what you say, here are a few tips on what you should practice, especially in regards to how you deliver your message.

Make eye contact

The person who is able to make eye contact with their audience will absolutely connect with their audience. Keep in mind that when practicing this technique, you must learn to make eye contact with more than just one person. If you are speaking in a group and only connecting with one or two people, those people will become a bit uncomfortable and your audience outside of them will become disconnected. What I like to do is look at the foreheads right between the eyes of people so it can look as if I may be talking to different individuals. I make sure to move around the room as well.

Speak clearly

There is nothing worse than coming to see someone who doesn't speak clearly and can't be heard. Make sure that you pronounce your words and speak up. You want to capture the attention of your audience. If you are mumbling, I can promise you they will lose connection with you.

Adjust your speech for your audience

This can be broken down in a few ways. One example of adjusting your speech may be to adjust your vernacular. You don't want to get in front of a group and use large words your audience doesn't understand. In fact, a rule of thumb is that the only time you would ever use specific jargon is if it is specific to that group. For example, if you are speaking in front of "techies" you may use technical terms. If you are in front of doctors, you may use medical terms. Another point for adjusting your speech is to base it upon location. I remember one time I was speaking in another country. I wanted to be able to capture the audience. This was my first time ever speaking in this country, and honestly, I was nervous as all get out. However, one thing I made sure to do was learn a little bit about the culture. So instead of doing my normal Introduction, I made sure to include something about their country. I even did my best version of their accent. When I did that, I was totally able to capture them because they knew that I truly cared about them. People will never care about what you know until they know that you care.

Another way you may have to adjust your speech could be based upon who you are speaking to. Again, the audience wants to know you care. Let's say that you are speaking to a group of real estate agents about your topic. Then you get a chance to speak in front of single mothers.

Your topic will still be the same, but you must remember that these are two different types of groups that you are speaking in front of. I may make mention of statistics in real estate when speaking in front of the realtor group, but not for the single mothers group.

How is it that I am able to adjust my talk based upon the group? I hope you've guessed it by now. Practice, practice, practice! When you practice, your base for your talk always stays the same, so if you have to add something in you can do so easily. Sometimes, if I want to add a new statistic specific for the group, I make sure to put the exact text within my PowerPoint, and if there is no PowerPoint, I'll read it from an index card.

Don't use one tone the entire speech

Learn to change your pitch when you are talking. If you have ever seen me speak, you know I can be a bit animated when talking. I'm not saying you have to do all of that, but do make sure that you change up your pitch.

If you ask a question, your voice will go up at the end because you are asking a question. If you are saying something that you don't want anyone to miss, like a quote, you may say it a bit stronger than your normal tone.

Think about a movie. A movie doesn't stay in one tone the whole time. Even the music is not the same. In fact, I'm sitting here as I write this book listening to Mozart, and what is so brilliant about this music is how the tone never stays the same. It's fast then slow, high then low. You want to be like a Mozart on that stage.

I am not saying try to become someone different. Just always work on being a better authentic version of yourself. One of the things I do is record myself doing my talk in order to pay attention to my tone. What you don't want to do is bore your audience, and this can easily happen with a monotone talk.

Don't belittle or call out your audience.
Never leave your audience feeling worse than when they came. I hope that whenever you talk, you have a goal to leave someone inspired. Regardless if it's inspired to buy your product or

service or inspired to change their life, you can't do it if you make people feel bad.

Let me give you an example. One time I was at a workshop and it was about finances. The speaker asked everyone to raise their hand if they currently didn't have any money in the bank.

A number of people were brave enough to raise their hands to say they didn't. The next thing the speaker did totally rubbed the majority of the audience the wrong way. The speaker went on to say that those who raised their hands were probably products of a broken home

Now there are just so many things wrong with this whole entire thing, but to start off with, you never have people raise their hands for negative things. You have them raise their hands for something that is positive or doesn't call them out. For example, the speaker could have asked for the audience to raise their hands if they had ever had a negative account. The next statement probably shouldn't have even mentioned that they were probably products of a broken home. If you've already had your audience already raise their hands for an embarrassing situation, the next thing is to provide a solution.

The best thing to ask yourself is, if you were in their shoes, would you want to be talked to the way you talk to your audience? No, I'm not talking about one-on-one coaching. I'm referring to people in a group setting. In one-on-one situations you are able to dig a bit deeper and expose more of this person's personal situations.

Also, never ever patronize your audience. Don't ask them a question and then say something like, "suuuure you did," with a tone like you don't believe them. For example, you may ask the audience, "how many of you have life insurance in here?" You already know the statistics. You know that more people raised their hands than what the average is. You don't have to call them out. You could just say something like, "Wow I am super excited and might I say proud we have this many people who understand..." Now for anyone who is lying, trust me, because you just praised them with a heart of genuine excitement, they will want to get the life insurance.

Be honest

I will say that one of the things most people say about me is that they appreciate how I am always being honest about life, business, and more. I don't mean being honest in the sense of getting on a stage and telling everyone all of your business and letting everyone know how hard life is.

No, I mean for example, let's say you are in network marketing, which as you know I was. Well actually you may not know that but I was and I earned multiple six figures in the industry in more than two companies. I would always hear these people get up in front of the group and make these false promises. This is why network marketing gets such a bad rep. When I got up to speak, I would always be honest. I would tell the success rate of the average independent distributor. I would talk about the work required. However, I would also talk about the benefits of the industry. This way people knew what to expect, and that's one of the reasons why my sign-up rate was always high.

The best thing you can always do is be honest. We are inundated with so much stuff today that it's like a breath of fresh air when you know someone is being honest about whatever it is they are talking about.

Organize what you're saying, especially in shorter talks

Most people think the longer the talk, the more you should practice. I will say that isn't necessarily true. I personally believe that the shorter your talk, the more you should practice. The reason is because you are given less time to make an impact.

I remember being hired to do a 10-minute talk. In most cases, I never accept a 10-minute talk opportunity unless it's a networking event and I'm a sponsor or something.

In a talk where I'm to deliver a true speech, I always require 30 minutes. However, for this one event I was being given 10 minutes, and honestly, I couldn't pass up on the offer because it was going to get me in front of some key influencers. For this 10-minute talk I probably practiced for 5 days, up to an hour per day. These 10 minutes were going to be amazing, and they absolutely were.

For longer talks it's easier, because I have more time. However, for the introduction and conclusion, I will typically practice those a bit more. Especially my introduction. Let's all be honest, we love to talk about ourselves, right? Well at least a large majority of us do. It's easy to get carried away sharing your story. However, keep in mind that the audience (in most cases) didn't come to hear you tell your story, they came to hear what you have to say in the body of your talk. The meat and potatoes.

The only time there is an exception to this rule is if you actually were brought in to tell your story but even in that situation your story must have a piece of it that will inspire or empower people.

Being visual with your hands is always great

I use my hands a lot. I may point at something on my presentation. I may have them open above my waist to bring people in. I make sure to use hand gestures when I'm talking to keep my audience engaged.

Now I know this can feel a bit weird if you are not used to using your hands. In fact, I know a lot of people love to use that darn podium to speak so they can hold on to it. I don't know about you, but the podium makes me even more nervous.

When you learn to use your hands when speaking, it will draw an amazing energy to you. An article I read from Dr. Carol Kinsey Goman, body language expert and author of "THE NONVERBAL ADVANTAGE: SECRETS AND SCIENCE OF BODY LANGUAGE AT WORK, and THE SILENT LANGUAGE OF LEADERS", on Huffington Post mentioned that, *"Hand gestures are really a powerful aspect of communication, from both the speaker's and the listener's end."*

Now I have a treat for you. Maybe you are still at a point where you don't know what gestures to use. I actually have some videos for you to see! Simply go to my website and you will see some videos on gestures you can use when doing your talks. The key to this is to practice your gestures so they don't look rehearsed. To check out this video, go to my website Bonus.SpeakingForProfits.com. Sign up there to get a series of emails to your inbox teaching you the proper gestures for success with your talk.

Chapter 21: Should I Prepare Shorter Versions? How Long Is Too Long For A Presentation?

All of my speeches are modular, meaning they all consist of 5-10 minute chunks. This makes it easy to memorize, and easy to remove or add pieces at the last minute or even as I'm talking. When I get booked to speak, I simply look at my portfolio of hundreds of 5-10 minutes pieces (some funny, some stories, some content, etc.) and pick which ones I want to piece together.

You should always be prepared to cut your speech if you need to. And you need to know how to cut it even at the last minute. It's the nature of this business.

And NEVER go over your time. EVER. Clients hate it. Audiences hate it. And the other speakers who are now having to cut their speech because of you, hate it. It's hard to stay on time. Practice.

Wear a huge watch or bring a big clock for the stage.

How Fast Should I Speak?

You should speak a little slower than you usually do, and pause more often, especially if you have an accent that is not the same as your audience. You've heard your speech a thousand times. They are hearing it for the first time. They need time to hear it, comprehend it, and even think about it a little. Don't rush.

Practice your speech on a friend and ask them their opinion. Don't use your mother – she will usually just tell you that your hair would look better if you pulled it out of your eyes.

And don't be afraid to pause when you complete a sentence, and even more when you complete a thought – especially if it's a powerful one. Don't be afraid of the silence. Sometimes it can be your most powerful weapon.

Is It Okay To Read My Speech?

Nobody really likes to be read to. So, no, don't read the speech. It's better if it's memorized. But that's really hard for many speakers, and it might not even be necessary if you aren't a speaker by trade. You're not going to want to put in all that work. The happy middle ground is to practice reading your speech so many times that when you get up to read it to the audience, you aren't really reading it, even though you have it in front of you. That will keep you from losing your place, which is the most common problem with reading a speech.

I memorize most everything I do, but occasionally there's a 5 or 10 minute chunk I didn't have time to memorize. I will type it up in a very big font and put it in a black notebook. I bring a music stand with me and put the notebook on the music stand and use that instead of a podium. It doesn't really block you and the audience doesn't really notice it much. And you can see every word of your speech. I make the font really big so I can lower the stand to about thigh-level to make it even less distracting.

Try not to give your speech from behind a podium. A podium minimizes the experience that the audience has. If they see more of you, then you have more opportunities to do subtle things to keep it from being boring. If all you see is a head, it tends to become just a talking head. Hhhhhhmmmm. I wonder if that's where they got the word?

Chapter 22: Do You Have An Important Presentation?

Sleep

I remember I was watching air crash investigation that day on TV. Those who are not aware of this, it's a program where they investigate air crash.

In that particular episode, they found that the reason why that crash happened is due to a basic mistake done by the pilots.

The investigators were quite surprised that how experienced pilots like them could do this kind of a basic mistake. They found out the reason.

Investigation report said "one of the key reasons of this mistake is lack of sleep by the pilots the previous night. Yes, when they checked the schedule of the pilot, especially the main pilot, the captain, they found that the whole day he was flying and even he didn't sleep properly in the night. At the time of the accident, he was very tired and lacked energy.

Now sometimes going on the stage is as difficult as flying, in fact, more difficult. When we go on the stage we need energy.

This is exactly what we do when we sleep and when we sleep we restore energy. When we restore energy, next day morning we have suffecient energy on the stage.

Because remember one more thing, if we have a big☐

presentation or big speech or big talk we think too much about it. No matter how much stage time or experience we have, this thinking drains a lot of energy from the body.

That's why if we have not restored energy the previous night and we are losing energy because of thinking - by the time we reach the stage there's no energy left.

When there is no energy, you know what happens? The audience sleeps. How do I know? I've done these mistakes in my life.

So next time if you have a big presentation or speech make sure you sleep and restore your energy. So, the next day when you are on the stage, you are full of energy and that will help you to communicate effectively on the stage.

10. Public Speaking is Like Singing

I was in Bangladesh to deliver a talk. The event was a blend of speeches and two to three performance by singers and I noticed one very good band came on the stage. There were three people in that band and one by one everyone started speaking.

Now many times we have seen singers they speak for a few minutes before they start performing their songs. I noticed that when they were speaking, they were very nervous, they were not looking confident.

But when they started singing, Oh my God! they were completely different personalities. They rocked the stage. People were dancing on their songs. They were awesome singers.

But why? Why suddenly when they started singing they were completely different people. They were confident while singing but when they were speaking they were not looking confident on the stage.

The answer to this "Why" is very simple, because like singing even speaking is a learnable skill. They had learned singing skills, that's why they were confident while singing. They didn't learn speaking skills that's why they were not confident when they were speaking on the stage.

Public Speaking is a learnable skill, in singing, we learn sa- ra - ga -ma, we learn nodes. in speaking we learn body language we learn vocal variety and also we learn how to organize the content.

When we learn singing, we practice. In speaking also, we learn and we practice. Even if you learn singing, no one in one night can become a good singer. Similarly, no one can become a good speaker in one night. We have to learn and practice it again and again.

But you know what if you don't like singing it's okay, it's not going to spoil your career. But whether you like public speaking or you don't like it, if you want to be a leader you have to learn public speaking.

Chapter 23: Storytelling - The Compelling Narrative

You could genuinely cut the tension with a knife.

The morning was a six-minute set speech where everyone could prepare, use cue cards and practice. The afternoon was a different kettle of fish.

I was in the speaker's room with all the other entrants of a regional speech competition, and we were all waiting to start the impromptu speech section.

Each competitor would be given a topic with one-minute preparation to deliver a three-minute speech.

The sense of unknowing going into this made the room a very tense and nervous place, with the atmosphere intense; and here I was lying on my back, knees bent up in the sun waiting for right moment to chop the tension to pieces.

"So, which one of you is going to get second place and join me at nationals?"

Everyone in the room stopped and looked at me. A couple of them hesitantly laughed, while the rest tried to figure out if I was joking or arrogant.

I was neither. Having seen all their set speeches I knew that I would win because of one thing I knew I would be doing that the rest of them wouldn't.

Since the dawn of time, we have used stories to entertain, educate, and empower; to motivate troops into battle, pass on the journeys of our ancestors, and share humorous tall tales told over a beverage with friends and strangers alike.

They give many of us an identity. Take note of your conversations for the next 24 hours. What percent of your conversations involve a story of the past or future?

The results will amaze you. We spend a huge amount of time drawing pictures in the minds of others, using stories. We start a lot of interactions asking either about the past or the future.

"How have things been going?"
"What have you been up to?"
"Have you got much planned today?"
Once we get past the pre-programmed answers of 'good', 'not much', and 'busy, busy, busy', we often dive straight into a story. It always amuses me when people say almost as a reflex they are good, then dive into a story demonstrating the complete opposite.

Why do we use these stories? They allow listeners to draw a picture of the situation, relate if they have experienced similar, replicate the feelings someone felt, and build rapport. The exact same thing occurs every single day of our lives with television shows we watch, books we are read growing up, and movies we watch.

To keep us engaged they must tell an effective story.

Although we all do this effectively in different ways every day, you learnt in the last chapter when we are on stage this goes completely out the window.

"Hi, I'm Victor and today I am going to be talking about three things. My aim is to make sure I talk for the required time and cover off the key points. In no place during my talk do I plan to effectively use stories to illustrate my points, entertain you, or ensure everyone is engaged. For my first point..."

Everyone has an ego. No one cares about anyone more than themselves. We must learn to play to that. To do this you have to apply a commonly used acronym in business and marketing.

WIIFM which stands for "What's in it for me?".

This is what every one of us think when we listen to a talk. How does this apply to me, what will I get out of it, and subsequently, should I keep listening?

You have two paths you can take. You can quickly stroke someone's ego by showing them what's in it for them; or create what we call an open loop, which keeps them intrigued and asking, "Is there something in it for me?". Both will result in a more engaged audience.

This is one effective way of creating rapport. Rapport is creating a bridge between your ego (experiences, beliefs and values), and your audience's ego. An open loop is like the less annoying version of clickbait in the speaking world.

We have all come across some sort of click bait article on a site at some stage; one that creates intrigue and a mental itch that needs to be scratched.

"This Is Why You Shouldn't Try To Outrun A Bear"

"Why Are You Single?"

"This Is What Happens When You Reply To Spam Email"

"At First, I Felt Sorry For The People Who Live In This Tiny House. Then I Looked Closer... Now I'm Jealous."

These are all actual articles on the internet right now. I will give you a minute to run off and close those loops.

Ever watched reality TV? They are the king of this. They give you a glimpse of something dramatic that occurred. Then comes the "stayed tuned after the break". These open loops keep you hooked to stay around until after the break, or ensure you are hooked for the next episode.

When a task, idea, or message is presented to us where there is a solution or outcome, our brains remain focused on it until we can close it off. This was first noted by a group of academics while having lunch one day. They remarked how amazing it was that the waiter was able to remember all their orders without writing anything down.

He reported to them once they had all been served (closing of the loop), he would struggle to remember the orders. This led to much research on the topic over the years with consistent results. When we are taken away from a task before completion, our mind remains fixated on it.

Think about your daily lives. You wouldn't decide to stop watching a great movie that has you captivated half way in. Imagine you got called away when your favourite sports team is in the final, all tied up with ten minutes to play. Your mind will be anxious to know the result and close that loop.

When possible, this is what you want to create with your stories. Opening and closing loops is an important aspect of storytelling, but just like The Public Speaking Blueprint, there is a framework for it.

This has been around decades, and more formally explained first by Joseph Campbell in 1987. Once you understand it, you will start noticing it in all your favourite shows, movies, books, storytellers, and speakers.

It's commonly referred to as the Hero's Journey.

The journey involved a likable character who discovers a desire for something greater. To reach this desire they must overcome some type of conflict. This is the character either moving away from pain or towards pleasure and can often be a mix of both. Every hero needs to have certain characteristics displayed in your story to truly define them as a hero. This makes them relatable to the audience and builds rapport.

Russel Brunson, who is an amazing speaker and one of the best at using the hero story in his presentations, uses the following steps to build up the likable character:

- Make the character a victim of some outside force, so we want to root for them.
- Put the character in jeopardy so we worry about them
- Make the character likable so we want to be with them
- Make the character funny so we connect with them

- Make the character powerful so we want to like them.

At the start of this book, I attempted to turn myself into this likable character. I was the victim of outside forces, by the peer pressure of my friends to bungee jump, and then being pressured to enter the speaking contest.

Sharing my physical and mental jeopardy by throwing myself off a bridge or failing to deliver a good speech was designed to make me likable and relatable; as many people can relate to being paralysed by their fears.

I won't comment on the attempt to make me funny, but hopefully it was woven within the story.

Setting the scene and developing the character makes it easy to see the conflict that must be overcome and resolved to get to the hero's desire. Conflict helps create the emotions you want your audience to feel. This is how you control the narrative.

Think of some of your favourite movies that we know aren't real, but still make our eyes water with emotion. Just to be clear, this doesn't have to be sad emotions. The conflict could be to win, escape, or stop something. To conquer this conflict, the hero must change their old beliefs to overcome the conflict and creating a new set of ideals. These new beliefs form part of your overarching message you want your audience to walk away with.

Start jotting down some stories from your life that highlight important messages and see how you can craft them to have open loops and tell a hero story.

You see, having sat through all the morning speeches, a couple of things stood out to me. A few of the speakers had obviously practiced their talk a lot; they had memorized it and gave an above par performance.

The other thing that struck me was that none of them could control a narrative.

They didn't effectively use stories and characters to shape their talk. Having seen this time and time again, I knew they all lacked a framework for the afternoon impromptu section.

So, were my earlier comments arrogant? No. I was confident that no matter the topic, I would be able to adapt, find a story, and convey a message.

Were my comments a bit cheeky when the rest of the room was already in a panic? Probably. Did my framework work? I'm not going to let you close that loop.

Just kidding.

I was the first one up that afternoon and got to see all the other competitors after me. I would have loved to be a fly on the wall after I walked out to hear what they said about me. Instead, I was out there killing it on stage.

A couple of hours later I received 1st place and a ticket to the National junior speech maker of the year finals.

Chapter 24: Influence The World One Speech At A Time

In the past, public speaking proved to be an effective venue for developing leadership and effecting change to individuals and the society. It is therefore not impossible to change the world one speech at a time.

At present, you should realize that the applications of public speaking have already been expanded. It is now being used in the commercial setting, in the corporate context, youth sector, and volunteer movements. Additionally, in the individual level, public speaking can be used to further enhance a person's self-confidence and professional development.

Speaking in Public to Influence others

It's high time for you to see public speaking as a means to make an impact in other people's lives. It is also privilege to move their hearts and influence their manner of thinking. If you are a leader of a certain group, public speaking can be seen as a strategy to persuade your subordinates and to motivate them to work towards your intended goal.

In the past and at present, it is safe to say that there is a high correlation level between the capability to speak well in front of a large audience and the capability to lead a large group. At present, as in the past, leaders are chosen not only because they do well in what they do; most of them are selected because they have an innate capability to speak their minds out effectively. Therefore, if you want to be a leader someday, you should hone your public speaking skills. It should be in your skill set. Note that most presidents of democratic nations were able to secure their respective seats because they can speak well.

By definition, leadership is a process that involves influencing the society by eliciting support and aid from other interest groups and from the people who are being led. Of course, capability to do intimate dialogues is important too. But if you wish to make maximum impact at once on as many people as possible, you should learn how to speak well in front of a large group.

If you know how to speak well, you can achieve the following: (1) unite people to work on the purpose that you have set; (2) create pressure (the positive type) on a group of people; (3) uphold the standards of excellent performance; (4) create team spirit and an atmosphere of cooperation and trust; and (5) drive people towards creating meaningful collective action and obtaining positive results.

Winston Churchill, Martin Luther King, Jr., and Nelson Mandela have one thing in common: they all have great public speaking skills. They are modern-day rhetoricians and orators who were able to fight with their speeches alone. They made names for themselves and a big impact on the society by merely delivering great speeches that tackle issues of the society during their days. They may be gone physically, but their ideas remain written on the pages of history – all thanks to their outstanding public speeches.

Now, more than ever, the society needs orators and public speakers who can be as intelligent and as courageous as King, Churchill and Mandela. The good news here is that you can always start with yourself. By studying closely the techniques discussed here, you are off to a promising start!

You are more blessed than the orators of the past because you have technology on your side. You can watch the television to watch public speeches. You can download the full text of their speeches via the Internet if you want to study the points that are worth emulated. With that, you can work on improving your public speaking skills.

Influencing the World despite your Humble Background

Technology has changed the platform for public speaking. Have you heard of that college sophomore whose freshman welcome speech became viral? That's an example of how you can influence the world despite your humble background. If you have something significant to say and you know how to say it in an interesting manner, you can try uploading it in a video sharing website. That way, you can share your thoughts, mold public opinion, affect people's emotion, and ultimately, change the world in your own little way. You have in your hands the access to the large audience – something that people in Aristotle's time were just dreaming for!

How to Influence others in the Context of Daily Living

You need to practice constantly so that you will be able to acquire the self-confidence that you will need in order to face a big audience. Also, if you will try to deliver your message to an actual audience, you will successfully conquer your fears. That way, you give your audience the opportunity to assess the merits of the ideas your present, the level of truthfulness that you and your speech bears, and the manner of organization that you have employed. And this can be a great way for you to learn.

More importantly, you need to learn the art of effective listening. According to experts, people who are capable of listening are the same people who can speak well. If you want to be a great rhetorician, you should know how to look out for logical points, emotional appeal, and ethical approaches in the speeches you hear. You have to be a critical listener if you want to be a critical speaker.

Conclusion

Congratulations. You have taken your first few steps to build confidence in public speaking. Take note, first few steps. As you gain more experience you will eventually build your confidence. Work with your fears gradually until you have conquered it to a level that can be easily managed or controlled.

You now have the tools with you to help you identify the depth of your anxiety, how to prepare for your talk to reduce your anxieties, how to cope with anxieties when they attack right in the middle of your presentation, and how to deal with the fear and not just treating the symptoms.

With experience your fears will melt away. May you exude confidence and candor in your next public speaking engagement.

www.ingramcontent.com/pod-product-compliance
Lightning Source LLC
Chambersburg PA
CBHW072002070526
44583CB00015B/1292